FIGHTING FOR JOY IN THE IN-BETWEEN

52 Prayers & Praises for Women

PEYTON HOFFMAN

gatekeeper press
Columbus, Ohio

FIGHTING FOR JOY IN THE IN-BETWEEN
52 Prayers and Praises for Women

Published by Gatekeeper Press
2167 Stringtown Rd., Suite 109
Columbus, OH 43123-2989
www.GatekeeperPress.com

Library of Congress Control Number: 2022936859

ISBN (paperback): 9781662927515
eISBN: 9781662927522

Printed in the USA

Faithful

I know that you'll be Faithful,
Once again, you will prove True.
So guard this weary heart of mine,
Lord, as I lift it up to you.

I praise you in this moment,
Tears streaming down my face.
You're breaking down these Jericho Walls,
And pouring in your grace.

I lift my eyes above the waves,
And listen for the roar.
Of the Lion who has rescued me,
And is restoring me once more.

These promises are yours to fulfill,
To protect and to defend.
So, I rest my heart here in the One,
Who is Faithful to the end.

—Peyton Hoffman

For my Eternal Father—through Whom
all blessings really DO flow.

And, for Dawn, Brooke, Gina, Dawnielle, Tara, & Heidi-Marie
—who first encouraged me to share these words with other women
and without whose prayers & constant encouragement this
devotional would never have been created.

Table of Contents

. . .

Introduction

• • •

For everything there is a season, and a time for every purpose under heaven:
a time to be born, and a time to die; a time to plant, and a time to pluck
up that which is planted; a time to kill, and a time to heal;
a time to break down, and a time to build up; a time to weep, and a time
to laugh; a time to mourn, and a time to dance; a time to cast away
stones, and a time to gather stones together; a time to embrace, and a
time to refrain from embracing; a time to seek, and a time to lose;
a time to keep, and a time to cast away; a time to rend, and a time to sew;
a time to keep silence, and a time to speak; a time to love, and a time to hate;
a time for war, and a time for peace.
Ecclesiastes 3:1–8 (ASV)

I NEVER INTENDED to write a book. Growing up, I always enjoyed writing but would consider myself an accidental author. At least before 2020. Because then you see, a global pandemic happened, and in the midst of what felt like constant change, I found myself swapping daily prayers via email with a group of Christian women. As the months went on, the Lord began using this time to lead me towards specific words and prayers for the in-between seasons of life. This was the beginning of this book—my email devotions as we walked through "the in-betweens" together.

We spend *a lot* of time in the in-between, witnessing a promise fulfilled in one area while hoping and praying for another. Maybe you feel like you're there right now, asking God why you're waiting, or why something hasn't happened yet, or what's next. Maybe you're asking the Lord to transform you, or, like King David, maybe you're believing for the Lord to show up and show out in your life. If so, sweet sister, this was written for you.

Here's the thing: the in-between is purposeful if you have eyes to see it. The in-between is that place of transition and transformation while the Lord is taking you from glory to glory. It might look and feel like stagnation, but it's not. This is where it's vital to dig deeper, believe longer, and move in faith. This is the refinement and preparation. It will stretch your faith far beyond that which you think you can handle. It will ask you to lay everything at the foot of the Cross. It will grow your patience, persistence, and perseverance like nothing else. Tears of weariness and shouts of frustration are intermingled with gratitude and shouts of joy in this place. It's a beautifully desperate place of the heart because it's where we come to the end of ourselves over and over again. And it's exactly where God loves to start before bringing us into someplace new.

The point of the in-between is to learn and grow so that we can be ready to step forward and elevate. Whatever the "new thing" is that you're believing for, it's going to require a higher version of you. Don't drop out early or stay too long. It's a place we return to multiple times throughout our lives, as the Lord enlarges our tents. So don't be upset to be here. This is a good thing. You want to be prepared for the next place and new thing. If you go there unprepared, what's meant to be a blessing will instead become a curse. You won't be ready to handle it. So welcome to a season that has a very specific reason. Let the Lord grow you, change you, and stretch you until He determines it's time to move forward.

In addition to lessons that, I believe, can only be learned in the in-between, there are also battles that must be won. One of the greatest battles we face in this season is the fight for joy. The joy of the Lord is our strength, so it makes sense that it would be one of the greatest things that the enemy comes after. By making us joyless, we become weak. When we become weak, we can be taken out by despair, weariness, exhaustion, or doubt. We lose sight of why the in-between season was created and instead get wrapped up in fighting the same fights over and over.

I believe that will not be your destiny, beautiful one. You will fight the battles here because this is where you learn *how* to fight—God's way. This is where you learn how to take the land that was always meant to be yours. As you start to see victory in the small areas, you'll start to believe for more. You'll need to lay some things down, build some things up, war well, walk in peace and praise before the breakthrough. You'll also need to receive revelation from the Holy Spirit to know exactly what to do and where to go. There are things that the Lord wants to say, instructions, blueprints for the future, guidance, and even core identities He wants to redefine. Whatever you believe about yourself is more than likely much, much less than what God believes about you.

This is for the woman who knows she's been living less than who she's been created to be. This is for the woman who knows she has to fight for her future but isn't entirely sure how. This is for the woman who's ready to see God be faithful. This is for the woman who is ready to start believing for more. And, if you are reading this, beautiful one, this is for you.

This devotional by no means covers everything about the in-between seasons, but it highlights some of the more prominent themes. I've left room for you to jot down your own prayers, praises, or notes each week if you want. Read the weeks in the order that they're written, or just flip to any week that jumps out. Whenever you can, speak the prayers out loud.

My prayer is that the Lord will use this to move your heart, draw you closer to Him, and unveil all that He wants to show you. That you would be incredibly blessed and emerge from this time with deeper confidence in the Lord. It will be worth it. There is more, beautiful one. There is so much more.

—Peyton

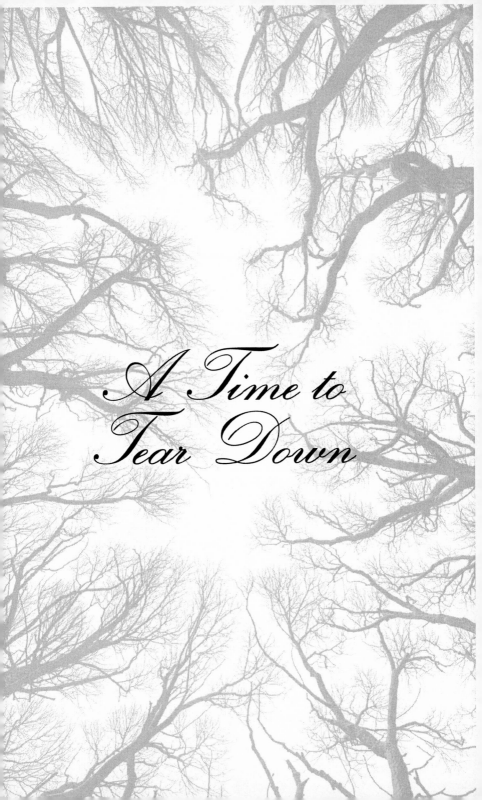

A Time to Tear Down

First Things First

• • •

Matthew 6:33 (NIV)
But seek first his kingdom of God and his righteousness, and all these things will be given to you as well.

Psalm 37:4 (NIV)
Take delight in the Lord, and he will give you the desires of your heart.

Revelation 2:4 (AMP)
But I have this [charge] against you, that you have left your first love [you have lost the depth of love that you first had for Me].

WHEN WE FIRST become Christians, everything is exciting. You know that you know that you know that God is real and has incredible plans. There are amazing revelations that keep the fire of that pursuit going. And then as we begin to mature in faith, the Lord begins using words like "Wait" or "Not Yet" or "I'm preparing you," and that's when it gets tricky. Keeping that passionate love for the Lord alive is one of the biggest challenges in the in-between seasons. Because when it's taking months or years for a promise to manifest or a prayer to be answered; when you're not only where you were, but also not where you know you are going, it's easy to grow weary.

One of the things that I love about the verses above is that they are all actions that must be taken by us. "Seek first," which means it's possible to "seek third" or "seek tenth" or not seek at all. "Take delight," which means that it's possible to lose or simply forget our delight in the Lord. It's also possible to place our joy and focus on something or someone else. "Left your first love" means we've done the walking away, the turning back, not God. We've abandoned the passion, the zeal, the curiosity, the flat-out awe that we had at first. It's a subtle rejection of the Lord as LORD. The deep hurt that we, as women feel, when we are overlooked, taken for granted, or rejected is just a tiny glimpse into the aching heart of God. When we are honest with ourselves and the Lord about what's really sitting in first place, the Holy Spirit comes in and brings us back to our first love.

The in-between places give us space to take inventory of our lives. To reset and realign with the One who made us and His direction for our lives. It's a place to take anyone or anything else that is holding position number one in our lives and remove it. It's a place where the Lord returns to His throne in our hearts. We cannot move forward in the in-between places without a firm grasp on the One who is leading the way.

Heavenly Father, we praise You today. Forgive us, Lord, for anything that we've put before You. Forgive us for losing the passion and awe that we once had for You. Holy Spirit, breathe on the embers of our hearts today, so that they may become a wildfire of love for You. Thank You that the in-between is just that—the space from here to there. Remind us that this season is for a specific reason. Teach us how to steward it well and how to keep moving forward. Help us, Lord, to truly delight in You so that our hearts may beat in sync with Yours. Reset our priorities in ways that only You can. Grant every woman reading this increased wisdom and discernment as we take inventory of our lives. Bring us back to our first love, out of which all other love flows, in Jesus's name. Amen.

Reflect

. . .

What's truly first in your life? Is it a job, a spouse, a child, a dream, or a certain status? Is it validation or approval from others? Is it an accomplishment? Is it money or lack thereof?

_____

_____

_____

_____

_____

_____

Where do you need to ask the Holy Spirit to come in and become first in your life?

_____

_____

_____

_____

_____

Which areas of your life need to come back to your first love this week?

_____

_____

_____

_____

_____

Put Isaac on the Altar

• • •

Genesis 22:1–2, 5, 16 (MSG)

After all this, God tested Abraham. God said, "Abraham!" "Yes?" answered Abraham. "I'm listening." He said, "Take your dear son Isaac whom you love and go to the land of Moriah. Sacrifice him there as a burnt offering on one of the mountains that I'll point out to you." . . . Abraham told his two young servants, "Stay here with the donkey. The boy and I are going over there to worship; then we'll come back to you." . . . "I swear—God's sure word!—because you have gone through with this, and have not refused to give me your son, your dear, dear son, I'll bless you—oh, how I'll bless you!"

RECENTLY, A WOMAN asked me, "Are you willing to put your Isaac on the altar?" It made me gasp. Not just because both the Lord and a trusted Christian confidante had already asked me. But because deep inside I wanted to cry out, "No!" Would I be OK without this? How would I even know when I'd placed this on the altar? She reassured me that, like Abraham, when I'm at the top of the mountain placing my Isaac on the altar, I would know. The Lord had repaid Abraham for every sacrifice, but this was different. This was the son through whom the Lord had promised Abraham's future. The one he loved. And like Abraham, because our Heavenly Father desires to be the focus of our hearts, we will be tested here in the in-between. We will be asked to lay down what's most important to us, in order to intentionally choose Jesus.

To become who we are created to be, to fulfill our God-given callings, it will cost us everything. Somehow, we've forgotten that the Lord asks for nothing less than everything from His people, over and over again. We may or may not need to physically move, but we will definitely part with some places, spaces, and people. We will be asked to lay all of our dreams and hopes on the altar. We will give it all to God. In order to receive beauty, we will have to let go of the ashes. In order to receive joy, we will trade the mourning that has kept us company for so long. And we'll know when we've put our Isaacs on the altar because it will wreck us to do it. To choose faith over the fear of loss and the Giver over the gift. Releasing our grasp in order to cling to God's heart more than His promises will not be easy. It's time though. Time to decide that God is not just good, but *the* good from which all good is birthed.

Months before, I wrote the words, "I will be with you as I was with Abraham" in my journal. Reading these verses now, the words leapt off the page. Abraham wasn't on the mountaintop alone and neither are we. In the sacredness of giving the promise back over, the Lord is there. He's with us as we choose to keep believing despite how impossible it looks or feels. Abraham knew he was coming back down the mountain with Isaac. He just didn't know how. What the Lord has done, He will do again. The in-between may be the place where we put it all on the altar, but it's also where we come back down the mountain knowing the Lord is truly Jehovah Jirah- the Lord our provider.

Lord, we trust You. We need You. Only You can do this thing. Only You can fulfill Your Word. Please, Lord, get the glory from this. We choose You and believe You are good, and You have only good plans for us. Almighty God, we know You will use this for our good in ways that we can't yet see. Thank You, Holy Spirit, for being with us as You were with Abraham. We cannot climb this mountain or lay our hearts on the altar without Your help. Please give us strength. We love You more than the gifts and promises. Lord, take all the praise. Keep purifying our hearts. Please give us fresh eyes to see You more. Make our lives a gorgeous reflection of Your love and faithfulness, in Jesus's name. Amen.

Reflect

• • •

What or who is the Lord asking you to place on the altar? Are you willing? Why or why not?

_____

_____

_____

_____

_____

_____

What do you think the Lord is working out in your heart through this?

_____

_____

_____

_____

_____

If you knew that you'd be blessed on the other side of this, what would you do differently?

_____

_____

_____

_____

_____

_____

Shut the Door

• • •

1 Peter 2:9 (NIV)
But you are a chosen people, a royal priesthood, a holy nation, God's special possession, that you may declare the praises of him who called you out of darkness into his wonderful light.

Isaiah 22:22 (AMP)
Then I will set on his shoulder the key of the house of David; [w]hen he opens no one will shut, [w]hen he shuts no one will open.

A COUPLE NIGHTS after I became a Christian, I dreamt that I was in a cave. In front of me was an open door, on the other side of which was complete darkness. And in that darkness were eyes, blacker than black, ravenous, but unable to cross the threshold to reach me. Between me and the door, sitting with his back to me, was an old man in a wheelchair. I froze—completely unable to move and close the door. As if hearing my thoughts, the old man asked, "Do you want me to shut the door?" I replied logically, "You can't. You're in a wheelchair." Unfazed, he asked again, "Do you want me to shut the door?" With increasing panic, I said, "How?" It looked impossible. The old man then turned his face partially towards me and said, "Peyton, do you want me to shut the door?" I realized that even though I didn't think he *could*, I really hoped he *would*. I let out a barely audible "yes," and with that, he stood and crossed the room to the door. He was suddenly neither handicapped nor old—in fact, he seemed much more alive than I was! Calmly, but with full authority, he looked directly into the eyes waiting in the darkness and said, "You cannot have her. This one is for good." And with that, he shut the door.

There are some doors that only God can shut and many doors that only God can open. Some doors close because they aren't good for us, others because that season has ended. In order to move through the in-between places, things will have to be laid down, released, or closed off. In any case, the closure is to move us forward, ahead, toward something better. This is not a punishment. It's the beginning of a breakthrough.

On the other side of this awaits an open door. It is a door to a life that's somehow beyond us, yet perfectly sized for us by the hands of Jesus. A door to dreams fulfilled and promises manifesting, to glorifying God with our every breath. But before we can reach that, we have to allow the old doors to be closed. Our job is to say yes to the shutting even if it's in a whisper. The old ways of doing things aren't going to work in the new places that the Lord is taking us. There are some old influences, habits, and even some people that will have to go because they will keep you from where the Lord is trying to take you. This is a painful thing, but a necessary thing. Whisper "yes." Start walking toward the unknown. It will be worth it.

Everlasting God, thank You for the doors that You have shut in our lives. Thank You for protecting us from more than we could ever know. We are so grateful, Lord, that this is by Your power alone. Jesus, You hold the keys of David—shutting doors that no one can open. Forgive us, Lord, for acting like limitations exist when there are none for You. We say yes to the doors that need to be closed and yes! to the doors that are ready to be opened. Thank You, Lord, that You have set us apart. Remind us, Holy Spirit, that we have been called for good. We praise You, Lord, for moving us toward more of Your love, Your glory, Your faithfulness, and the incredible unfolding of Your promises. You have never stopped working. Thank You for calling us out of darkness and into Your incredible light, in Jesus's name. Amen.

Reflect

• • •

Is there anything the Lord is asking you to walk away from or doors that need to be shut? What's been keeping you from taking that step?

_____

_____

_____

_____

_____

Which doors have you not allowed the Lord to open? Where is the Lord knocking on your heart, asking you to let Him enter in?

_____

_____

_____

_____

Which doors are you believing for the Lord to open in this season?

_____

_____

_____

_____

_____

Make Space for God's Grace

. . .

Psalm 84:11 (TPT)
For the Lord God is brighter than the brilliance of a sunrise! Wrapping himself around me like a shield, he is so generous with his gifts of grace and glory. Those who walk along his paths with integrity will never lack one thing they need, for he provides it all!

IN THE SUMMER of 2019, I walked into an AIDS clinic in South Africa as part of a short-term mission trip. There was no agenda other than to spend time with people and love them. I knew that there was a holy weight to this, but I never could have prepared myself for what God was getting ready to do.

Everyone else had peeled off to chat with patients in the room. Looking around, I saw a woman in a bed by the corner. She was the only one still alone. I practically skipped over to her, having already decided she'd be my new friend, and introduced myself. As I spoke, I watched her lift up her hands and signal something. Oh no. She was deaf. I didn't know sign language. How would she know she was loved? With the questions still in my heart, I felt wrapped in a warm blanket. Opening my mouth to speak, my hands started moving too. Her eyes widened like saucers. And then she responded. That's when it hit me that I was signing. She understood me and I understood her. And it wasn't weird. She told me that she used to be in a deaf clinic but had come to one for AIDS patients. She was sad because it was far from home, and she'd lost her Bible. We happened to have some brand-new Zulu Bibles in the back of our van, so I grabbed one. Before I could even offer it, she snatched it out of my hands and started rocking back and forth, sobbing. It was as if I'd just given her air to breathe.

The medical staff commented on how great it was that the Americans brought someone who knew sign language, only to learn this was all Holy Spirit. I heard later that in the month she'd been there, I was the first person who had communicated with her. All it took was a little less agenda; a little more room for God to show up and show off. I have no doubt that the Lord brought me all the way from California to South Africa so that this beautiful daughter would know that she's seen and loved. I have no doubt that He wants to use us to be awe-inspiring vessels of His love.

Make space for the Lord to show up and show off. Hold agendas and plans loosely. The Lord has more for us in the in-between than we have for ourselves. He wants to stretch us beyond what our eyes have seen and what we think we know. He wants to use us to continually let others know how much they are loved by Him. We need the Lord's grace more than we could possibly imagine, and others need to see it through our lives. If we make the space, He will usher in his grace, glory, power, and love.

Heavenly Father, none of Your children are deserving of Your grace and yet, we are growing and becoming stronger in spirit with Your favor and blessing upon us. Reveal to us, Holy Spirit, the areas in our lives where we need to make space for Your grace. Transform our minds and hearts into new wineskins for Your grace and glory. We give You our areas of influence, time, and yes, Lord, even our very purpose on this earth. We ask that You would cover it with the blood of Jesus. May our words and actions be vessels for Your grace to reach this hurting world. Holy Spirit, we ask that You would shine the power of Your light through our lives. In Jesus's mighty name, we pray. Amen.

Reflect

. . .

Where do you wish you had more of God's grace in your life today? What's filling that space?

_____
_____
_____
_____
_____
_____

Where do you find yourself placing limits on God?

_____
_____
_____
_____
_____

What needs to be cleared out this week to make room for the Lord to move in?

_____
_____
_____
_____
_____

Holy Ground

. . .

Exodus 3:5 (AMP)
Then God said, "Do not come near; take your sandals off your feet [out of respect], because the place on which you are standing is holy ground."

1 Corinthians 3:16 (ESV)
Do you not know that you are God's temple and that God's Spirit dwells in you?

WHEREVER THE Lord is, is holy ground. We know this, and yet, we forget. With God living in us through the Holy Spirit, that means that we are on holy ground whenever we are in community and relationship with other Christians. When we share our hearts, our stories, our dreams, our fears, our hopes with one another—we are on holy ground.

If we're honest with ourselves, we don't always treat others (especially those we may not agree with) as if who they are, what they say, and the cries of their hearts are holy ground. If we're even more honest, we don't always treat ourselves as if there is holiness inside of us. We don't handle others, or ourselves, with gentleness or sacredness. We haven't always been women who give others a safe place for their hearts to land. We can be dismissive when we should be leaning in. We're quick to forget that these interactions are a gift and an extension of God's trust in us.

We all fall short here. How easy it is to rush through a conversation like a to-do list—trying to check the box instead of quieting our souls and listening with love. Our human nature makes it easy to be "me first" instead of "others first," but that doesn't make anyone feel special or valued. Our culture tries to convince us that we're missing out, so we answer calls or text messages instead of making the person in front of us the most important conversation. And we're tempted to treat those who we agree with as somehow holier than those who we don't. But that's not how God works. He uses every person for His purposes, which means that there's something for us to gain from everyone around us if we are humble enough to see it. How quickly we forget that every interaction is a chance for the Holy Spirit to shine and for us to learn.

Fortunately, there's the in-between, where the Lord rebuilds His house within us. To do that, the old, weaker, lesser things must be torn down. The fire of holiness is reestablished within us. This place is where the Lord holds up a mirror to show us where we've forgotten the sacred things. It's where our hearts are purified so that we're prepared to step into more. The ground beneath our feet was once the ceiling of someone else's prayers. The heights of our faith will one day become the new foundation for those who follow us. It's time to look around with eyes wide open and recognize the holy ground again.

Heavenly Father, You alone are worthy. Lord, we have all fallen short in honoring one another and in turn, in honoring You. We have failed to recognize when we are on holy ground with each other. Our heart's desire is to listen and love one another well, but we desperately need Your Holy Spirit's help. Quiet our souls. Alert our spirits when we start to get careless. We need ears that hear what isn't spoken as loudly as what is. We need eyes that see Your sacred, unfailing love. We need more of Your wisdom, Lord. May we become women whose lives have come through the fire of holiness. Help us to acknowledge the awesome privilege and responsibility You entrusted us with when You gave us the gift of community. Jesus, we love You. Amen.

Reflect

• • •

Are you aware of when you are on holy ground with others? How do you treat others in those moments and how do they treat you?

_____

_____

_____

_____

_____

_____

What are some ways that you can handle interactions with others differently this week?

_____

_____

_____

_____

_____

Which areas of your life need to be made holy by the Lord?

_____

_____

_____

_____

_____

Take Up Your Mat and Walk

. . .

John 5:2–9 (NIV)

Now there is in Jerusalem near the Sheep Gate a pool, which in Aramaic is called Bethesda and which is surrounded by five covered colonnades. Here a great number of disabled people used to lie—the blind, the lame, the paralyz- ed. One who was there had been an invalid for thirty-eight years. When Jesus saw him lying there and learned that he had been in this condition for a long time, he asked him, "Do you want to get well?" "Sir," the invalid replied, "I have no one to help me into the pool when the water is stirred. While I am trying to get in, someone else goes down ahead of me." Then Jesus said to him, "Get up! Pick up your mat and walk." At once the man was cured; he picked up his mat and walked.

HERE WAS MERCY in human form, at Bethesda (the house of mercy), offering mercy, and the man missed it. This man didn't even say that he wanted to get well. When Jesus asked him if he wanted to get well, the guy made excuses! Did he not think Jesus could help him? Or had he believed the lies for so long that he'd lost sight of the truth? It's easy to read this and judge, but how many of us have been lying at the foot of the house of mercy for years in our own lives? How many of us are waiting for healing in one form or another—spiritual, emotional, mental, physical, or relational? And how many of us have grown used to the lies telling us that things won't change?

This mat had become part of the man's identity—a reflection of what was wrong. It was how he was known by others, and how he identified himself. He'd been there, waiting for his miracle to come for so long that he didn't even recognize it when it arrived. Why didn't Jesus just have him leave the mat behind? I believe it's because that mat—that reminder of his former identity—helped others immediately spot the greatness of his transformation. What if the man had never picked up his mat and walked as Jesus commanded? He was cured by the words of Jesus but could've continued lying on his mat, never walking (literally) into his answered prayers. Jesus spoke the healing into existence, but the man still had to get up!

You and I are going to have to do something. The enemy does not want to see the plans of God fulfilled in our lives and is banking on us staying paralyzed. Lying on the mat is where we hear lies like, "This is never going to change,'" or "Just give up—it's too hard," trying to convince us that we should just stay where we are. But it's also where Jesus asks, "Do you want to get well?" It's time to listen to Jesus over everything else. He is the same yesterday, today, and forever. He has not stopped healing, and if He asks us to pick up our mats, it's so that people can see that we're the real deal. Our mats become our ministry through Jesus. So today, beautiful one, it's time to pick up our mats. It's time to listen and obey. It's time to let the new thing begin.

Holy Spirit, show us the mats that we've been lying on for days, months, or even years. We pray that You would make clear to us exactly which mats it's time to pick up this week. Thank You for calling us forward into wholeness, healing, and answered prayers. Thank You, Almighty God, for allowing us to partner with You—for giving us a step of faith to take. Help us to lay down all of the things that might hold us back. We ask, Lord, that Your glory and Your healing power would shine through us. We pray, Lord Jesus, that others would see the changes in us and praise You! Amen.

Reflect

• • •

What is the "mat" or "mats" that the Lord is telling you to pick up and move?

_____

_____

_____

_____

_____

_____

Why are you still "lying by the pool of Bethesda" when God is calling you to walk?

_____

_____

_____

_____

_____

_____

Where does the Lord want to turn your mat into your ministry—changing your mess into His message?

_____

_____

_____

_____

_____

_____

Count the Cost

. . .

Psalm 121:1–2 (TPT)
I look up to the mountains and hills, longing for God's help. But then I realize that our true help and protection is only from the Lord, our Creator who made the heavens and the earth.

A FEW YEARS back, I had the opportunity to hike the Tour du Mont Blanc—a 101-mile circuit through the French, Italian, and Swiss Alps. We started out before dawn and daily summited a different mountain, before returning to eat and sleep about twelve hours later. Day one, my mind told me there was no way I was going to climb all these mountains. It was too hard. It was too high. I hadn't trained enough. Day two, I was reassessing everything I'd brought along. This was no time to be carrying extra stuff. Day three, the tiniest muscles in my arms and legs—ones I didn't know existed—hurt. Day four, I was exhausted. But by day five, I'd found a good rhythm. By day six, it hit me that I was actually doing this! By day seven, I was telling people it wasn't bad. And by day eight, I couldn't wait to go again.

Like a mountain climb, so goes the in-between. We need an expert, trust-worthy guide. One minute we're on a solid road, and the next we're climbing on our hands and knees over diagonal slate rock that's hanging over a cliff—literally and figuratively. We have not been this way before. We don't know the best path. Our guide had hiked that circuit hundreds of times—earning the right to tell us where to step, how to climb, and when to slow down, or even stop. He reminded us that the higher we go, the less baggage we can carry. So it goes with God. The Lord has walked this path. He may take things away, so that we carry only what's necessary. If that happens, it's so that we don't give up along the way. It will get harder before it gets easier. It will take longer that we thought it would and use muscles we didn't know we had. And, unlike the bottom of the mountain where there may be a crowd, only a few will make it to the top. The Lord will strip people away as we elevate because not everyone has the preparation, the calling, or the sheer desire to go higher. Not everyone is meant to go where we are going. And that's OK. That said, we cannot get to the top alone. We will all need a few women who have been this way before, because there will be times when we have to silence our minds and simply keep walking on autopilot. And in those moments, they will spur us on and keep us going.

So, count the cost. And then go all in. Because our Guide created those mountains that look imposing from the valley. He'll help us climb them and then will give us others to follow after us. We will do more than we thought possible, and the adventure will be amazing. We will believe for the transformed places before we reach the mountain's peak. We will remind ourselves that every instruction is for our good. We'll let others help us along the way. And when we finally get there, standing at the top of the mountain, we'll discover that even the deepest, darkest valley has become breathtakingly beautiful.

Lord, lift our eyes up to You, so that we look above the mountains that are in front of us. Holy Spirit, You promised to guide us, never letting us stumble or fall. Almighty God, You are our keeper; You never forget or ignore us. Everlasting God, fulfill every ounce of Your word in our lives. Come close and be at our side once more to lead us safely through this place with Your Presence. You are the Lord our Protector, keeping us from every form of evil or calamity as You continuously watch over us. Show us the view from Your perspective. Help us to not only believe for, but also see the valley transformed when we reach the mountaintop. We believe You're worth it, Lord, and we believe Your Word, in Jesus's name. Amen.

Reflect

• • •

What mountains are standing in front of you right now?

_____
_____
_____
_____
_____
_____
_____
_____
_____

Where do you need the Lord to guide you in taking that next step?

_____
_____
_____
_____
_____
_____
_____
_____
_____

Who are the women around you that are climbing higher with you? Who's on your team?

_____

_____

_____

_____

_____

_____

_____

Which mountains have you already climbed that you can see others following behind in your path? What encouragement can you give them this week?

_____

_____

_____

_____

_____

_____

_____

_____

_____

_____

_____

_____

_____

_____

Abide Don't Strive

. . .

John 15:5 (ESV)
"I am the vine; you are the branches. Whoever abides in me . . . bears much fruit, for apart from me you can do nothing."

Luke 10:41 (NRSV)
But the Lord answered her, "Martha, Martha, you are worried and distracted by many things."

LAST YEAR for Lent, the Lord asked me to give up striving. Seriously. Not chocolate or social media. Striving. Here I was, aware that every amazing thing in my life was because God had held fast to His promises, yet utterly convicted. How had I started striving? And how had I not noticed?

The shift is subtle. It's when doing for God replaces being with God. There was nothing inherently wrong with Martha preparing a meal for Jesus. She probably had done that before. After all, Jesus was close friends with Martha, Mary, and Lazarus. But this time, it was a distraction. She was missing out on the blessing of His presence—a blessing that was actually for her! When doing *for* God lifted her eyes *from* God, something had to change. It's the same for us today.

In the in-between places, there's always something that isn't happening as quickly as we want, or in the way we thought. We take our eyes off of Jesus and start to see ourselves as the answer. We try to "help" God by fixing things that were never ours to fix. In reality, that's pride and doubt, plain and simple. God doesn't need our help. The Lord asks us to partner with Him, as a way to bless us and grow us, but He definitely does not need our help. You think Jesus couldn't have just spoken and given Martha a meal? He's the very WORD that brought life into existence.

Abiding in the Lord, the exact opposite of striving, is what we were created for as women. It is a gift—a place of renewed devotion and passion. It's saying, "Lord, I don't even *want* anything apart from you." It's setting our eyes back on Him and letting our hearts rest there. It's letting the quiet that's within us drown out the noise that's around us. The practice of abiding takes intent for everyone, but it's worth it. Personally, I had to start saying no to some opportunities and literally set aside time with the Lord on a calendar. And, you know what? It worked. The more I would abide in the Lord, the more I actually wanted to abide with Him! My heart and soul started growing for more of the kingdom, and with it, my capacity for joy increased. As a bonus, I received instructions for things that were to come that I didn't even realize I was going to need. Rest here, beautiful ones. Abide and let God do it.

Heavenly Father, thank You for showing us exactly where we each need to focus right now. Thank You for reminding us that apart from You we can do NOTHING, so it's truly laughable to try. Help us to remember that Your promises are Yours, and Yours alone to fulfill. Forgive us, Lord, for trying to take the reins back into hands that are too small to hold them. Thank You for always being more ready to give than we are to receive. You are immeasurably Faithful and True. Holy Spirit, I pray that You would place a check on our hearts, so that when we are tempted to strive, we'd stop and give it all back to You. Help us remember that abiding is a gift from You, and one that we are worthy of receiving through Jesus. Help us to not strive or delay the promises You are fulfilling in our lives. Soften our hearts to lean into Your Holy Spirit even more so that we can change into the women You created us to be. Amen.

Reflect

. . .

Where have you found yourself acting like Martha lately?

_____

_____

_____

_____

_____

_____

_____

_____

What situations, relationships, or dreams have you been tempted to "help" God fix?

_____

_____

_____

_____

_____

_____

_____

_____

_____

_____

In what ways might those very actions be delaying the answers that you're looking for?

_____

_____

_____

_____

_____

_____

_____

_____

_____

Where is the Holy Spirit nudging you to hand over the reins once more? Are you ready?

_____

_____

_____

_____

_____

_____

_____

_____

_____

A Time
to Build Up

Everlasting Arms

• • •

Deuteronomy 33:26–28 (CSB)
There is none like God of Jeshurun, who rides the heavens to your aid, the clouds in his majesty. The God of old is your dwelling place, and underneath are the everlasting arms. He drives out the enemy before you and commands, "Destroy!" So Israel dwells securely; Jacob lives untroubled in a land of grain and new wine; even his skies drip with dew.

Matthew 19:14 (ESV)
[B]ut Jesus said, "Let the little children come to me and do not hinder them, for to such belongs the kingdom of heaven."

I GOT TO VISIT family on the East Coast recently and spent time with my six-year-old niece and one-year-old nephew. For the first several days of my visit, the only place they wanted to be was wherever I was. If I was sitting in a chair, they both had to be sitting in it with me. If I was eating dinner, they both had to be eating next to me. Whatever room I walked into, they followed. Their pure little hearts and overflowing joy to just be in the same room as me was the most beautiful thing. It was such a sweet reflection of the relationship that our Lord desires for us. It made me think of how Jesus calls us to be like little children and how much we wander from that as adults.

This is where we begin to feel the arms of Jesus lift us up like little children, holding us close, and keeping us safe. It's where we find ourselves dancing without a care in the world and singing praises at the top of our lungs from somewhere deep in our souls. It's where our hearts want to leap out of our chests because we've heard the words "you are safe" from the only One who can hold that promise.

The most loving, unhurried, and unworried place for us to be is in the ever-lasting arms of the One who loves us, nurtures us, defends us, and provides for us. How much the Lord longs for us to be like little children—following happily from room to room of our lives instead of closing doors to Him. How beautiful our faces would be because each new place of our lives holds a new adventure with the most trusted Leader. How much the Lord longs for us to live untroubled while He provides for us all that we need, and then some. How much the Lord wants us to remember that we are safe. That we are wanted and adored—rejoiced over with singing and quieted with His love. The everlasting arms are the only ones strong enough to hold us and what-ever we're walking through at this very moment. These arms carry us when we are exhausted, embrace us when we are scared or sad, hug us when we need reminders of how loved we are, and lift us high in celebration and laughter.

Heavenly Father, thank You that You call us to Your everlasting arms. Hold us today, Lord. Holy Spirit, we come to You like little children and ask that You'd remind us today of the joy that's found in You. Jesus, it's only in running to You as little children that we begin to see Your kingdom come to earth. We trust You, Lord, and settle in to rest in You today. Only through You can we have childlike faith, childlike joy, childlike peace. You are our protector. You know what's best for us—far more than we can possibly understand. Help us today, Abba, to be unhurried and unworried because we are in the best place—with You. I ask for a special gift of peace over the women reading this. May they see a unique glimpse of how You are holding them close, in Jesus's name. Amen.

Reflect

* * *

How do you picture the everlasting arms of the Lord? Do you feel safe there?

_____
_____
_____
_____
_____
_____

If your life were a house, would you be excited to follow Jesus from room to room? Why or why not?

_____
_____
_____
_____
_____

Would you be willing to open every room to the Lord this week? What re-assurance would you need from the Holy Spirit to take that step?

_____
_____
_____
_____
_____

The Lord Who Goes Before You

• • •

Isaiah 52:12 (AMP)
For you will not go out in a hurry [as when you left Egypt, nor will you go in flight [fleeing, as you did from the Egyptians]; For the LORD will go before you. And the God of Israel will be your rear guard.

Psalm 139:5 (TPT)
You've gone into my future to prepare the way, and in kindness you follow behind me to spare me from the harm of my past. With your hand of love upon my life, you impart a blessing to me.

IN 2015, THE SPIRIT impressed on my heart that I would move to California. Having worked in tech, I assumed this meant Northern California and rushed to find a job there. That's when things got weird. I would be in the final stage of hiring, and all of a sudden, the budget was pulled, or a corporate hiring freeze rolled out, or someone left the company and the process had to start all over. Through no one's fault, the Lord firmly shut doors over and over until I finally "got it." I had to learn to get behind the Lord in His timing and ways so that He could fulfill the promise that He had given. He brought me into an in-between season to prepare me for where He was bringing me, which ended up being Southern California three years later. It was a time and a place that didn't make any logical sense, and yet, it was perfect. When I did finally move, it was with complete clarity and peace. The Lord brought me a job opportunity that had been created specifically for me. This repositioned an unhurried and unworried me within both a land—and a community—that was already waiting for me.

God is leading and leaving His footprints behind us right now. Like the Israelites, we won't have to flee. We will not be in a hurry. We will be led by the Lord with His hand of love upon our lives, surrounded and protected, as we move from the in-between into the new. We will remain until the Lord says to move. We will go peacefully. We will test and trust over and over. As we put one foot in front of the other, we learn to have faith for the path that we cannot see. We believe where we are headed because we trust the One who leads the way. As we follow, as we learn to let Him lead, we will find the Lord placing His hand of blessing on our lives along the way.

We must move at the pace set for us by the Holy Spirit, knowing that God Himself has already prepared the way. We cannot get ahead of God or lag too far behind. As we keep moving, the Lord will follow behind us to transform every single thing that's been left in our wake. Our God chooses to do this work Himself. Our futures matter so much to Him that no one else is allowed to create this beautiful transformation in our lives. He will brush away every piece of our histories so that they no longer interfere with our destinies. Our little footsteps of timidity transform into firm steps of powerful, confident assurance as the Lord goes before us into each new day.

Heavenly Father, we are completely in awe of You. Your majesty, Your healing power, and Your saving grace truly know no bounds. Who are we, Lord, that You would go before us—leading us with such gentleness, surrounding us with Your favor as with a shield, enclosing us in Your love? Who are we that You would go behind us—covering the echoes of our steps in this life with the glorious power of Your own? We don't want to go one day without experiencing how real You are. Help us to let You lead by listening closely, obeying quickly, and expecting great things to come. How amazing are Your desires for us! You know what we need much more than we know how to ask, so we pray that You would intercede for the unspoken things in our hearts and minds. Heavenly Father, please make us vessels of Your redeeming love by the mighty name of Jesus Christ. Amen.

Reflect

• • •

How great is God that He would personally go before you to lead and protect you? Where have you seen the Lord go before you?

_____
_____
_____
_____
_____
_____
_____
_____

Where have you experienced the Lord as your rear guard—protecting you from surprise attacks?

_____
_____
_____
_____
_____
_____
_____
_____

How merciful is God that He ensures that the footprints we leave on others' hearts and lives are swallowed up in His own? In what ways are you thankful that the Lord constantly covers the echoes of your steps with the grace of His own?

_____

_____

_____

_____

_____

_____

_____

_____

_____

What pace do you feel the Lord setting for your life this week? Is it to slow down and rest? Is it to speed up and press on?

_____

_____

_____

_____

_____

_____

_____

_____

_____

_____

Special Favor

. . .

Isaiah 61:1–3 (NIV)
The Spirit of the Sovereign Lord is on me, because the Lord has anointed me to proclaim good news to the poor. He has sent me to bind up the brokenhearted, to proclaim freedom for the captives and release from darkness for the prisoners, to proclaim the year of the Lord's favor and the day of vengeance of our God, to comfort all who mourn, and provide for those who grieve in Zion—to bestow on them a crown of beauty instead of ashes, the oil of joy instead of mourning, and a garment of praise instead of a spirit of despair. They will be called oaks of righteousness, a planting of the Lord for the display of his splendor.

Psalm 5:12 (NIV)
Surely, Lord, you bless the righteous; you surround them with your favor as with a shield.

WHEN I WAS thirty-two years old, my appendix ruptured. Only, I didn't know it ruptured. I was sick, but figured it was a stomach bug. Through a wild series of events, I ended up in the hospital two months later with doctors unsure of what was wrong. After two days and heavy antibiotics, I agreed to an exploratory laparoscopy and appendix removal if needed. That's when the general surgeon on the team was introduced, and I realized it was one of my best friends from high school. We had lost touch, and I didn't even realize she was a surgeon now. The surprise was mutual. I go by my middle name, which wasn't the name on my chart. It wasn't until after surgery that I realized that it wasn't random that she was there. The Lord placed her there as a sign of His favor. A twenty-five-minute standard appendix removal turned into a very difficult five-and-a-half-hour surgery.

The long-ruptured appendix brought many unanticipated complications, including my body calcifying itself to prevent infection from spreading to my heart, lungs, and brain. No one could've prepared for that. The Lord used this friend from high school to, quite literally, save my life. That is the favor that surrounds us like a shield. I believe that part of the reason for that friendship then was because the Lord saw this moment in my future. He prepared the favor in my youth that I would need in my life as an adult.

Think about all of the people in the Bible who had the favor of the Lord upon their lives: Noah, Ruth, Esther, Joseph, David, Daniel, Moses, and more come to mind. Each time one of them is specifically mentioned with favor from the Lord, it coincides with a unique "choosing" and purpose. There is a choosing and purpose for this favor upon each of us today. It may be provision or protection. It may flow through us to others, or through others to us, but it is unmistakable. The Lord wants us to experience His favor! If we look around, we'll see where people in our lives have been positioned for divine alignments and assignments. We'll understand that those we influence are not there by accident. In the in-between, we'll begin to desire to be the representation of the Lord's favor in someone else's life. We'll pray to see others blessed because of the favor that rests upon our lives. We'll start blessing as many people as we can, in as many ways as we can, for as long as we can.

Almighty God, thank You for surrounding us with Your favor as with a shield. Thank You for giving us so many examples of who is favored, how You call Your children favored, and why You call us favored. Thank You, Holy Spirit, that Your favor has a big purpose! Thank You that there is something for us to do with it—something bigger than ourselves. Today, we come before You to ask for more of Your special favor in our lives. Open our eyes to see the favor You are bestowing on us to flow through us. Help us to lean into Your Holy Spirit so that we can hear Your whispers. May we radiate Your light and glory to a confused, dark, and lonely world around us. Help us, Lord, to walk this well in Jesus's name. Amen!

Reflect

• • •

When have you seen the special favor of the Lord upon your life? What was the unique purpose in it?

_____

_____

_____

_____

_____

Who were you able to impact because of the Lord's favor that you couldn't otherwise have reached?

_____

_____

_____

_____

Where do you need a special portion of the Lord's favor this week?

_____

_____

_____

_____

_____

No Eye Has Seen

. . .

Paraphrased from 1 Corinthians 2:9 (AMP)
My eyes have not seen, ears have not heard and it has not entered into my heart (all that) God has prepared (made and keeps ready) for me because I love Him (I hold Him in affectionate reverence, promptly obeying Him and gratefully recognizing the benefits He has bestowed).

I HAD THOUGHT about moving to a different part of LA and found myself imagining my new home. I made a list of what I wanted—everything from the number and size of the bedrooms and bathrooms to more space and an open floor plan. I even listed renovations and a beautiful, safe neighborhood where I could take prayer walks as criteria. This was already more than what I had, and yet, I had one more thing on my heart: I would get this better place without paying a penny more than I did for my current home. It looked crazy. No one gets more for nothing in LA, and yet, that's what the Lord had put on my heart. Soon afterward, I saw a condo online and instinctively knew this was it. I was excited. There was no phone number, so I submitted my information only to hear . . . nothing. I kept trying to no avail. I looked at other homes, but something was always off. Plus, everything was more expensive than my current home, and that wasn't my promise.

Four months later, fighting off discouragement, I looked online again and—for the first time—saw a phone number. I called, toured the condo, applied, and was approved all within seventy-two hours. Not only did the place have every single thing I had listed—from the layout, to 400 additional square feet, to a beautiful neighborhood, to being completely renovated that month—but it also had amenities that I hadn't even thought of. It was listed at hundreds of dollars more per month than my current place, but the owners agreed to drop the price! I ended up not paying a dollar more than my current home and ended up with so much more! It was everything the Lord had promised and then some. And, while the delay was frustrating, I discovered later that it was that exact delay that paved the way for the renovations and price drop. When the Lord opened that door, the delay absolutely worked to my benefit—it just wasn't something I could see at the time.

The Holy Spirit wants to outdo our dreams. It's time to start letting promises of hope enter our minds and hearts again. It feels counterintuitive living in the in-between. Maybe we're believing for a job to get better when God wants to provide an entirely new career! Maybe we're believing for a marriage to become bearable when the Lord wants it to reflect His complete restoration and grace. Anything we can think up is not even going to come close to what the Lord has planned. As we see the Lord move in specific areas (finances, health, relationships, homes, etc.), it helps us to believe for greater things in other parts of life. Delay is not denial. When the Lord moves, even the delays will have been for our good and our victory. Start believing again and get ready to see great things unfold!

Heavenly Father, thank You that the little we can imagine or see or hear is just a tiny sliver of all You have planned for us by the power of Your Holy Spirit. Open our hearts and minds to see the new things You are doing. Please don't let us miss this, Jesus. We want to stay in step with You. May we be amazed today, Lord. Fill us with laughter, joy, and excitement as You start unveiling the things You have planned. Holy Spirit, I ask that these things would not only be a testament to us of Your goodness and glory, but also that it would testify to those around us of the unmatched greatness of our God. Holy Spirit, we can't wait to watch You work! Help us to get out of our own way and Your way, where we need to, so that You can do a flourishing work in our lives. Amen.

Reflect

. . .

What is the cry of your heart this week? Where would a surprise from the Lord increase your faith?

_____

_____

_____

_____

_____

What's something that the Lord clearly had prepared, but you didn't realize it until later?

_____

_____

_____

_____

How does this stir up your faith to believe that the Lord can and will come through for you once more?

_____

_____

_____

_____

_____

Nothing Is Impossible

. . .

Mark 10:27 (NIV)
And Jesus looked at them and said, "With man this is impossible, but not with God; all things are possible with God."

Luke 1:37 (ESV)
For nothing will be impossible with God.

WEBSTER'S DICTIONARY defines *impossible* as: "[F]elt to be incapable of being done, attained or fulfilled; insuperably difficult." Felt. How many times do we assess the possibility of something based on how we feel? Feelings aren't always the truth. Jesus didn't say, "With man, things are difficult," or "With man, things are frustrating." He said, "With man, things are *impossible*." Here's the thing about impossible. If we break it down, it actually says something very different.

Impossible. Im possible. I'm possible. I AM possible.

The possibility is right there, hidden in the impossible all along. What separates the *impossible* and changes it into something *possible* is the I AM. There is only one I AM and—spoiler alert—it's not us. God is the great I AM. We serve a God who delights in transforming our impossible into His possible! If we look at the world only through what we can do, we see barriers because the impossible was never meant for us to accomplish. We look around us for the answer, forgetting what the Lord has already placed within us. What if we are the impossible that the Lord wants to make possible? What if the seeds of our possibilities have been there all along? Let's take our eyes off of our feelings, off of what we can't do, and place them back upon the Lord. Let's start filtering what feels impossible through the reality of what God can do. We don't need faith for the possible. Impossible is the Lord's starting point, so that's not a place to get discouraged. The Lord will move, and when He does, things come together suddenly.

Abraham and Sarah had a baby when they were "as good as dead." Hannah was given a son when she was barren. Moses parted the Red Sea. Esther, an orphan, became queen so she could be positioned to save her people. Enoch was taken up into heaven without tasting death. Lazarus was called out of the grave and given back his life. Peter walked on water. Philip was teleported from the eunuch's chariot to Azotus. Paul was shipwrecked and bitten by a viper but wasn't harmed. The blind were given back their sight. The sick were healed. The lame walked. Jesus died on the Cross—and then rose again three days later. All of these things are impossible in the natural world, and yet, they all still occurred. The entire Bible is full of impossibilities happening, so why would it be any different for our lives today? There is nothing impossible for our God. Stand in faith. It's not over. God can still do it.

Forgive us, Lord, for looking at the illusion and accepting it as reality. Take our eyes off our circumstances, Lord—Off ourselves, our emotions, our limited understanding, and our ways. Place a lens of truth over our minds, our hearts, and our eyes, Jesus, so that we may see this world through what You can do. All creation exists because You called it into being so there is nothing that won't bend to Your call or Your will, Holy Spirit. Lift the veil from our eyes, Lord, and instead, reveal a whole new level of what's possible. Teach us how to walk by faith and not by sight. We love You and cannot wait to see what You will do, in Jesus's name. Amen!

Reflect

• • •

What looks impossible to you today? Now ask the Lord to show you how this looks to Him.

_____

_____

_____

_____

_____

_____

How does that change your perspective of what's in front of you?

_____

_____

_____

_____

_____

Where have you accepted that your current circumstances are permanent or lowered your expectations instead of pressing on for the Truth?

_____

_____

_____

_____

_____

Trusting God

. . .

Proverbs 3:5–6 (AMP)
Trust in and rely confidently on the Lord with all your heart, and do not rely on your own insight or understanding. In all your ways know and acknowledge and recognize him, and he will make your paths straight and smooth [removing obstacles that block your way].

Isaiah 26:3 (NIV)
You keep [her] in perfect peace those whose mind are steadfast, because [she] trust[s] in you.

I WAS DIAGNOSED with pediatric epilepsy in 1990. For as long as I can remember, my life has included EEGs, lab tests, and medications on a regular basis. As I grew older, conversation turned from "maybe you'll outgrow this," to "let's make sure it doesn't get worse." I became an adult living a high-functioning life with a pediatric neurological disorder. I didn't "fit" the normal path. "Keep doing what you're doing" was tossed around for years, until one day, everything changed.

In August 2021, my neurologist said the words I'd been waiting for: "There's no longer any evidence that you have the epilepsy you were born with." It was a physical healing thirty-one years in the making. Decades of getting my hopes up, only to see them tumble down. And though the healing was a "sudden" experience—one day I had the diagnosis that I'd known most of my life, and the next day I didn't— the process tested my trust in God for years. Simultaneously, it was the slowest and fastest process. I used to pray that things would stay status quo. That was a win. I couldn't diet and exercise my way to healthier brain waves. Healing wasn't even a conversation, yet in the back of my mind, it was always a hope. Looking back, I can say, with total assurance, that the Lord knew what He was doing. There were times in my life where this was actually a divine protection. Healing came exactly on time but differently than I imagined so that only God would get the glory.

I never imagined that I'd spend a week in an epilepsy monitoring facility under 24-7 observation that summer. I never pictured getting to talk about how God heals with medical staff in Southern California. I never imagined that playing worship music from a hospital bed for a week would minister to so many—that people would walk in commenting on how peaceful and joyful it was there. Or, that I'd hear whispers of "I'm believing for you" and see faith rise in complete strangers every day.

One of the biggest questions we have is "will God come through for me?" Sometimes it's easier to believe in the Lord's faithfulness for others than it is for ourselves. We know in our minds that God is faithful, and speak it, but can still be unsure in our hearts. Perhaps this is why the Lord reminds us that with all our heart we must trust Him. It's the things that hit our hearts that truly test what we believe. The Lord fulfills His word, beautiful one. Just because it hasn't happened yet doesn't mean that He isn't working things out in the background right now. God *is* trustworthy. Not was, not will be, but *is*. Today. In the middle of hopes delayed or dreams deferred. In the middle of the places where it looks like nothing is changing. Even here, God can be trusted. But the path will not look anything like what we plan. The Lord really is Who He says He is and can do all that He says He can do.

Forgive us, Lord, when doubt sneaks in, or when we are tempted to rely on ourselves—our own strength, our own knowledge, or our own timing. Increase our confidence in You, Lord. You are working. You are Faithful and True. You can be trusted, and You love us beyond measure. Help us to remember, Jesus, all the times You have come through for us in the past. May our eyes reflect hearts that are confident that You have not forgotten us. You are coming through for us again, now and always. Amen.

Reflect

. . .

Who or what are you trusting in your life more than the Lord?

_____
_____
_____
_____
_____
_____
_____
_____
_____

Why do you think that's been the case?

_____
_____
_____
_____
_____
_____
_____
_____
_____
_____

Where do you find yourself asking the Lord if He will come through for you?

_____

_____

_____

_____

_____

_____

_____

_____

_____

What is one thing you can speak over your life this week to remind your-self that God is truly, relentlessly for you?

_____

_____

_____

_____

_____

_____

_____

_____

_____

WEEK 15

Known

. . .

1 Corinthians 8:3 (CSB)
But if anyone loves God, [s]he is known by him.

Psalm 139:15—16 (NIV)
My frame was not hidden from you when I was made in the secret place. When I was woven together in the depths of the earth, your eyes saw my unformed body. All the days ordained for me were written in your book before one of them came to be.

MY FIRST MISSION trip took me to work alongside the Dalit people of India. It's shocking to see an entire population that is overlooked, not counted, and treated as sub-human. It's even worse if you're born a Dalit woman. The very word *Dalit* means broken or scattered and that's every bit of the definition of the lives I saw. On the other hand, it's also where I witnessed some of the most dramatic conversions to Christianity. I was fortunate enough to witness many Dalit baptisms—all of whom, subsequently, chose that day to celebrate as their birthdays. I discovered that many didn't know their actual birth dates, so they chose that day to be the day they were born. That would be a day they celebrated from now on. It's the most amazing thing to speak with Dalits who have given their lives to the Lord, because it's the first time they realize that who they are truly matters.

Everywhere we look, there are people struggling with feeling overlooked, unseen, not cared for, or simply unknown. Every single person has this inherent desire to know and be known because God wants to be known and we are made in His image. Just like the Lord wants us to get to know Him, we want to get to know those whom we love. We want to be seen and known by those who love us. To love is to know and be known.

The problem is that, as humans, we're afraid that if others really knew us, they wouldn't really love us. So, we hold back—from each other and from God. We fail to treat others and ourselves as if we were created on purpose and for a purpose. Trying to live on our own just leads to an emptiness, a hollowness, that nothing and no one but God can fill. So the Lord, in all His wisdom, gives us these in-between seasons that drive us closer to Him— where we get to know Him much more than we did before. We forget that we've been designed to live in unity with God and in unity with each other. The more we know the Lord, the more we are actually becoming ourselves! It's time to ask the Lord for more of His Presence. It's time to see who we really are, and why we were uniquely created and placed here, in this place and time. There are reasons far beyond what we can see, but it's time to realize that we, beautiful ones, matter. We are daughters who are seen by the Creator of the universe and known more fully than we can ever imagine.

Heavenly Father, You knew us before the creation of the world. You saw our unformed bodies and gave each of us unique personalities, gifts, promises, desires, and dreams. Help us, Lord, to remember that we are already fully known by You. Holy Spirit, it is only by Your power that we can walk out this kind of love in our lives. Give us promptings, nudges, words, images, anything You want Lord, to open the doors of hearts that feel unknown or unseen around us. We long to be vessels of light and life for You, Jesus. Help us to point others toward You in such a way that they can no longer question whether or not they are known or seen or valued. We lean into You now, Jesus. Place words of life on our lips this week, Holy Spirit, as we watch others turn back to You, Lord Jesus, may every person You bring across our paths feel deeply seen and uniquely known. May our hearts bring them closer to Your heart. Amen.

Reflect

• • •

Do you truly feel known? Seen? Or do you feel like you're existing in a world that looks right past you?

_____

_____

_____

_____

_____

Why do you think you are here at this time on the earth? Knowing that you were created with purpose, what are some of the unique aspects to you and your story that God can use?

_____

_____

_____

_____

_____

_____

_____

What's something you can do this week to make others feel seen and known?

_____

_____

_____

_____

_____

_____

Jehovah Shammah

. . .

Psalm 139:7–10 (NIV)
Where can I go from your Spirit?
  Where can I flee from your presence?
8 If I go up to the heavens, you are there;
  if I make my bed in the depths, you are there.
9 If I rise on the wings of the dawn,
  if I settle on the far side of the sea,
10 even there your hand will guide me,
  your right hand will hold me fast.

YEARS AGO, I WAS riding in the car, not really paying attention, when suddenly I found myself listening to the driver tell a story about my life. Only this person didn't know it was about me. I was suddenly listening to my life, and my mistakes, as if it were juicy gossip. And in that moment, I had two thoughts: (1) God might be real, and (2) If God was real, I was in big trouble. Because at that time, my life was a dumpster fire on top of a disaster wrapped with a ribbon of rebellion. Somehow, by the sheer grace of God, this conversation broke through. It was like the Lord took a magnifying glass to my heart—to the broken places that all of that had grown from—and said, "Enough."

Three nights later, at two o'clock in the morning, I pulled my car over on the side of the road and said, "Lord if you're there and if you hear me and if you have time, I need you to take this away. I need you to remake me because I can't do this on my own." It was the prayer of a child's heart—of a daughter coming home—and in that moment, I gave my life to the Lord. The Lord had been there all along, waiting with abounding patience for me to come back. He not only removed that thing from my life within three weeks, but He has also answered that prayer a thousand times over since then. Not everyone has to have a dramatic conversion in order to know that Jesus is real, but I did. When a heart has grown hard, or cold, or rebellious, the breaking is actually where mercy begins. That's where I met Jehovah Shammah.

This name of God, referenced at the end of Ezekiel, means, "The Lord is there." It's spoken by Ezekiel to the Israelites, when they are at their worst, their most idolatrous moment, as a promise of restoration. God would return to Jerusalem and remain with them. Oh, beautiful ones, that promise is not just for the Israelites. It's for us! This is real. True restoration—wholeness and holiness—is better than anything this world can offer. When we ask the Lord to return, He promises that He will remain with us, and we with Him. It's the most beautiful promise and it will change your life. I know Jehovah Shammah. I have seen the goodness of the Lord in the land of the living, and it is *so good*. The Lord is in the Promised Land, yes, but He's also in the in-between. He's in both the process and the completed restoration simultaneously, and if it can't be restored, it will definitely be redeemed.

Father God, You alone are Jehovah Shammah. Thank You that the future You have in store for us is a plan for good and not disaster. Thank You, that You are a most patient God, extravagant in love and always ready to cancel catastrophe. Please do not remove Your hand of protection from us, Lord. We love You and we need You. Thank You for already standing firm in all of our tomorrows. We bind any spirits of anxiety, fear, or shame that may come against Your daughters in the mighty name of Jesus right now. We send them to the foot of the Cross, where nothing can stand in the presence of Your Holiness. May we not give a single second of our energy to things that do not align with Your nature. May Your kingdom come and Your will be done, on Earth as it is in Heaven. Amen.

Reflect

• • •

How much are you like the Israelite people of Ezekiel's day?

_____

_____

_____

_____

_____

_____

Where do you need a reminder that the Lord is "there"?

_____

_____

_____

_____

_____

Where are the places that you've been fleeing from the Lord? Where do you need Him to hold you and bring you back home?

_____

_____

_____

_____

_____

Obedience Is Love

. . .

John 14:15–17, 21, 23 (NIV)

"If you love me, keep my commands. And I will ask the Father and he will give you another advocate to help you and be with you forever—the Spirit of Truth . . . Whoever has my commands and keeps them is the one who loves me. The one who loves me will be loved by my Father, and I too will love them and show myself to them" . . . Jesus replied, "Anyone who loves me will obey my teaching. My Father will love them, and we will come to them and make our home with them."

I'VE BECOME RELENTLESS about obeying the Lord. It is one of the ways that the Lord has sharpened my ability to hear His voice and be blessed. I've come to realize that obedience is a litmus test for Christians. It is an active response to hearing God—regardless of how we feel, or what we think we know. The saying "actions speak louder than words" is what Jesus is getting across here. Obedience shows that we believe in the ultimate goodness, sovereignty, power, and authority of God. It means that we believe in who God is more than what He gives. Obedience shows that we believe that everything God tells us to do or not do is ultimately for our good. Because God is Love, every command given to us is from love and in love. It's to protect, guide, help, heal, save, transform, reassure, and encourage us.

It's tempting to look at obedience to God as something that limits us, and to an extent, it does. Because we were never created to be our own gods, and in a fallen world, we desperately need the Lord's leading for our own protection. Obeying God is a tangible way to show that we trust His ways and timing more than our own. It is a constant form of remembrance that God is in control, and we are not. As we consciously and consistently obey God, our faith increases. We become more patient (waiting on the Lord) and grow in wisdom. The connection between obedience and love is the very foundation of what it means to show honor, which is why of all the ways that we could show love, Jesus picked obedience as the defining factor of His followers. Jesus didn't say, "If you love me, you'll understand my commands," or "talk about my commands," or even "you'll always want to follow my commands." He said, "Anyone who loves me will obey my teaching."

As we step out in obedience to the Lord, we'll be given instructions that don't make sense. I've found myself at 6:00 a.m. prayer—walking around a specific place seven times, bringing down Jericho walls in the Spirit. I've driven to a church I'd never heard of to receive a breakthrough I didn't know I needed. I've sat next to a stranger who ended up being a pivotal divine alignment for my life. I've prayed over a pastor from my childhood and watched the Lord bring him physical healing. And there's so much more. In each of these things, I only received a piece of instruction. Never the why. We discover the reason why after we obey—never before. And whether it's something that's meant to happen to us or through us, it's always a blessing for us. And if we step out and we're wrong, that's OK too. That's how we learn how to hear the Lord's voice more clearly. We don't lose out when we obey. We test and try, like the Israelite priests sticking a foot in the Jordan River before it would part. And we watch God move mightily.

Heavenly Father, help us to be quick to listen, slow to speak, and eager to obey Your Voice. Grant us discernment to know when You are speaking and help us to not listen to any other voices. Holy Spirit, remind us that Your commands are for love and from love. Thank You, Jesus, that we were never created to be our own gods. Thank you, Abba, for giving us Yourself, so we'd always know where to go, what to do, and who to follow. Lead us clearly this week so that our lives may gain new ground for You. Amen.

Reflect

. . .

Why do you think Jesus lists obedience as one of the things to do to keep from falling away?

_____

_____

_____

_____

_____

_____

Where do you feel the Lord asking you to obey this week? What are you being asked to do?

_____

_____

_____

_____

_____

Are you ready to ask the Lord to give you clear opportunities to obey Him this week—no matter how small or strange it may seem? Why or why not?

_____

_____

_____

_____

_____

_____

A Time
for War

Speak Life

. . .

Ephesians 4:29 (TPT)
And never let ugly or hateful words come from your mouth, but instead let your words become beautiful gifts that encourage others; do this by speaking words of grace that help them.

Proverbs 12:18 (TPT)
Reckless words are like the thrusts of a sword, cutting remarks meant to stab and to hurt. But the words of the wise soothe and heal.

WE LIVE IN A WORLD that bombards us with negativity everywhere we turn. From the news to social media, we see a culture yelling inadequacy, insecurity, doubt, shame, and death to women. We see bitter hearts speaking words that sting with jealousy, grudges, or conflict; critical hearts spewing disparaging, demeaning words; self-righteous hearts hidden behind judgmental words; and thankless hearts under nonstop complaints. Not everything in life is life-giving. This is not who or how we were created to be.

Part of the preparation in the in-between is learning the power of our words. We've been called to speak life and must surround ourselves in this season with others who speak life into us. Not everyone has earned the right to speak into our lives. We were created in the image of God, Who spoke this entire world into existence. Our words have the creative power to transform our environment. Speaking life is first and foremost to speak in agreement with the Word of God. This is part of how we war—intentionally speaking life instead of death. This time, this place is where we learn to speak life, regardless of what's going on around us. If we can't speak life in this place, we won't be able to get to the larger, open spaces that are waiting for us. There are giants in the Promised Land, so even after we step into what is for us, we will have to displace them. And we will do that with the words of life that we learn to speak now, in this time and in this place.

The Bible is full of life-giving words that remind us of who we are. Hearing words spoken out loud with our own ears is how we gain confidence and combat the enemy. It brings victory. Speaking life transforms our minds and our hearts. A bitter heart becomes a loving, trusting heart that's full of gracious, uplifting words. A self-righteous heart becomes a contented heart that's full of faith-filled words. That heart becomes humble, filled with words of acceptance, reconciliation, or restoration. It becomes a joy-filled heart full of words of gratitude and thankfulness.

We are the righteousness of Christ in Jesus. We are daughters of the King—a royal priesthood. We will live and not die. We will be strong and mighty in the land. We are the head and not the tail, above and not beneath. We will lend and not borrow. We will laugh at the days to come. Our children will arise and call us blessed. Let's become women who start agreeing with the Lord's promises!

Forgive all of us, Jesus, for speaking out of bitter, thankless, self-righteous, or critical places. Lord, transform us into ones who speak life out of the abundance of our hearts, so much so, that those around us would begin speaking life in agreement with You as well! May we be the small pebble that begins a ripple effect of life-giving change across our neighborhoods, our cities, and our nations. Holy Spirit, we need You. We cannot do this well or consistently without You. Do not let us be led by our emotions, or the circumstances around us, but by You and You alone. May we be women who speak validation, gratitude, honor, and encouragement. We ask You to do for this world what only You can do—take us from death to life in the mighty name of Jesus, our Lord and Savior. Amen.

Reflect

. . .

What's something that you've been complaining about that can be re-framed into words of gratitude?

_____

_____

_____

_____

_____

_____

What situations have caused you to speak death instead of life this week—words of bitterness, fear, or insecurity, instead of peace, unity, and love?

_____

_____

_____

_____

Where do you feel a check in your soul—your mind, will, emotions and spoken words—to begin building others up instead of tearing them down? Who specifically comes to mind?

_____

_____

_____

_____

_____

Silence the Roar

• • •

1 Peter 5:8 (MSG)
Keep a cool head. Stay alert. The Devil is poised to pounce, and would like nothing better than to catch you napping. Keep your guard up.

Revelation 5:5 (NIV)
Then one of the elders said to me, "Do not weep! See, the Lion of the tribe of Judah, the Root of David, has triumphed. He is able to open the scroll and its seven seals."

I VISITED A WILDLIFE sanctuary in South Africa a couple years ago. Riding in an open top, windowless jeep, we entered the lion enclosure and stopped in between a male lion and two lionesses. The lion, lounging in the sun and licking his giant paws, couldn't care less that we were there. The lionesses, however, were very interested in our presence. It was then that our guide turned his back entirely to the male lion and, facing the lionesses, explained that they're the silent, deadly hunters. When the lioness fixes her gaze, it shifts her into "hunt mode" and unless her gaze is broken, she'll pounce. So whenever either lioness began to fix her gaze on us, our guide walked over and whacked the lionesses on the top of their noses! It was just enough to break their concentration, cause confusion, and make the lionesses forget to hunt.

This is the exact same thing the enemy tries with us. We hear the roar of fear and want to run. But the wild pack of shame, offense, bitterness, and inadequacy is lying in wait to tear us apart. In turning away from the noise, we actually turn our faces toward more danger! Fear causes us to look at the situation and forget to really see. Breakthrough, redemption, power, and fresh anointing lie ahead, which is exactly why the noise is meant to scare us off track. That's why it's so important for us to fix our gaze on the Lord and on what's beyond the noise. It's in leaning into the roar that we access the redemption, the healing, or the promises that lie beyond it.

Remember that the roars of the enemy are only *like* a lion. The power of the real lion is inside of us, so roar back! Like David ran toward Goliath, go toward the noise in the power of the Lion of the Tribe of Judah. Silence the loud shouts of shame, guilt, rejection, despair, disappointment, and fear with authority bought by the blood of Jesus Christ. As we pray and move in faith, we do more than whack our enemy on the nose. Everything flees when we let loose the roar of Holy Spirit across the earth. In the in-between, when the enemy gets loud—trying to scare us off course—just remember Who really knows how to roar. Don't be afraid to use this weapon! The roar of the Word of God is the roar that silences all others, and we can access it every day, anytime we want!

Almighty God, Lion of the Tribe of Judah, we worship You! Holy Spirit, remind us that we fight from victory for victory. May we stand when You say to stand and run when You say to run. Stir our hearts up with courage and strength even now, Lord. Thank you for using all things for our good and Your glory. Holy Spirit, we are in complete awe of how You choose to work through us and simply ask for more of You in our lives. Help us to be women who live and love fearlessly. Place in our hearts Your Word that silences the roar of all others. Abba, may we have eyes to see all that You have uniquely prepared for us in Jesus's name. Amen.

Reflect

• • •

What if that roar of offense or rejection is actually the open door through which God will draw someone to Himself?

_____

_____

_____

_____

_____

What if that roar of fear is the very place that God desires to bring break-through?

_____

_____

_____

_____

What Truth can you speak over your life this week to silence the roar of the enemy?

_____

_____

_____

_____

_____

Refiner's Fire

. . .

Jeremiah 23:29 (AMP)
"Is not My word like fire [that consumes all that cannot endure the test]?"
says the Lord, "and like a hammer that breaks the [most stubborn] rock [in
pieces]?"

Proverbs 25:4 (AMP)
Take away the dross from the silver, And there comes out [the pure metal for]
a vessel for the silversmith [to shape].

1 Peter 1:7 (AMP)
[S]o that the genuineness of your faith, which is much more precious than
gold which is perishable, even though tested and purified by fire, may be found
to result in [your] praise and glory and honor at the revelation of Jesus Christ.

GOLD IS A SOFT METAL, so it commonly contains other metals (lead, iron, copper, etc.) before being refined. Those other metals harden the gold and decrease its value. The refining process is incredibly intricate and time-consuming. It's no surprise that it's been proven to be up to twenty times more accurate than any other method of refinement. It starts by assessing how much of the gold is pure gold, then separating out the impurities. In order to do that, the fire is heated to between 1,832- and 21,632-degrees Fahrenheit, turning the metal into liquid. The gold sinks to the bottom and collects together. The impurities float to the top and are removed. The gold is then heated and purified a second time—this time to remove any silver from it (which collects with the gold during the first purification). The end result is pure gold.

I love that the pure gold is there all along and must go through the process of refinement more than once. The initial refinement process removes the things that are toxic in our lives or in our hearts. The second (or third or fourth) process isn't to remove impurities as much as it is to remove something that's good but less valuable (the silver). How much we are like this gold, full of areas that need to be removed to leave behind only what's best. Just because something is good doesn't mean that something is of God. It is not our future to continue to be wrapped in impurities and less-thans.

This is the fiery process of the in-between. We are supposed to be tested and approved by fire. And yet, we feel the heat and want to avoid it all. We want microwavable gold from a God that refines by fire. We get upset if we go through this process more than once but it's to purify us, not destroy us. Don't fight the fire that brings victory. All that is impure or of lesser value in our lives must be burned away. We are placed in the heat because the Lord wants the pure gold that's inside to be all that remains. Pure gold is almost transparent, so as we become women of gold, others look at us and see the heart of God.

Thank You, Heavenly Father, that whether we come to You as scrap gold—with years of impurities built in—or raw gold—young and fresh from the mountain, You welcome us with open arms. Thank You, Holy Spirit, that no matter how high the heat, this makes us who we were created to be. Almighty God, we embrace the refining fire today. You promise that this work results in praise and glory and honor at the revelation of Jesus Christ and we want that! We embrace Your handiwork in us. Make us into dazzling jewels for Your Kingdom. Thank You for hammering away the hard places, for making us soft again, and for removing the impurities in our lives. Thank You for repeating this process until You see the reflection of Your own face in ours. Lord, give us words to encourage others in the refiner's fire. Amen.

Reflect

. . .

When's the last time you can remember being in the refiner's fire? What did it feel like?

_____

_____

_____

_____

_____

How is the Lord using situations in your life right now to soften you, to chip away at the hard places, or to remove anything/anyone of lesser value from your life?

_____

_____

_____

_____

How is this transforming you?

_____

_____

_____

_____

_____

Worship Is Warfare

• • •

Lamentations 3:22–24 (NIV)
Because of the Lord's great love, we are not consumed, for his compassions never fail. They are new every morning; great is your faithfulness. I say to myself, "The Lord is my portion; therefore I will wait for him."

I FOUND MYSELF at church this morning saying, "Lord, I just need a tangible reminder of your faithfulness this week." And here's the thing: I know God is faithful. My life is nothing but evidence of the faithfulness of God. Yet, here I was on a Sunday morning with circumstances and feelings trying to tell me something different. So what did I do? I worshiped. I stood there and let my worship become warfare. I praised God and cried and prayed until my feelings caught up with my faith. And I didn't care who saw because I needed the Lord to break though like only He can do. And He did.

Worship is more than songs sung on a Sunday morning. It is a lifestyle. We were created to be in worship with our Creator at all times. In this fallen world, worship often goes elsewhere—to things or people but we still worship, all the time, because that's what we were created to do. Music postures our hearts and minds in adoration but that's only the beginning. It's not where worship ends. Worship is more than kneeling, though kneeling positions us in humility and servant-heartedness. Angels, the twenty-four elders, and the four living creatures all fall down on their faces before the one true God as is written in Revelation, and we will too.

Worship is the only thing we bring to the Lord that He didn't first bring to us. Everything we have is because the Lord gave it first, but the Lord never worshipped Adam and Eve nor will He worship us. Worship is we, the created ones, asking the One who is Holy and Sacred to take hold of that which is holy and sacred to us. To do this, we embrace, even if only for a moment, the love that casts out all fear. We still our hearts and remind ourselves that the Lord will step in and do more than make wrong things right; He will make all things new. This is our act of sacrificial love to the One who *is* sacrificial love. No enemy can stand in the presence of this. This is when our worship becomes warfare.

Praise is powerful. And when we truly understand that concept, we will want to live a life full of true worship. Bringing a sacrifice of praise to the Lord, especially when it doesn't match what we see around us, brings the invisible into the visible and literally changes the atmosphere around us. When we lay our souls on fire at the feet of Jesus, it draws out of us a strength, a boldness, an awe, a love, a joy, a humility, a trust, or an adoration that reflects a heart of worship. The Lord picks these pieces up and wars for us. Every time we praise God for the breakthrough, for the promise, for the restoration, the healing, the redemption before we see it occur, we are claiming victory in the spirit. As we remind ourselves that our worship is powerful, it defeats the enemy. We declare a little bolder, sing a little louder, kneel a little longer, and watch as our God is faithful once more.

Almighty God, all glory and honor and praise is Yours. Help us to war in worship. We trust You, we love You, and we believe You, Lord. By the power of the Holy Spirit and in the name of Jesus, we place into Your hands right now the loved ones, the situations, the hopes, the desires, and the promises that were always Yours to hold. We acknowledge right now, Lord, that only that which is truly Sacred, You and You alone, can handle that which is sacred to us. This is our offering and we lay it all before You gladly! Bring us, Your created ones, into a new awareness of Your love and desire for us. Stir us up in awe, in adoration, in humility, in love, in reverence, in joy, and in song so that we can be all that You have created us to be. Send us out into the world to do what You have created us to do, walking in Your love that casts out all fear by the power of the Holy Spirit and in the name of Jesus. Amen!

Reflect

• • •

When you picture what it means to live a life of worship, what does that look like to you?

_____

_____

_____

_____

_____

_____

Do you think living a life of worship is really possible? Why or why not?

_____

_____

_____

_____

_____

Where do you want to see the power of worship increase or change your life?

_____

_____

_____

_____

_____

Becoming "How Will" Women

. . .

Luke 1:34 (NIV)
Mary [when she was told she would give birth to Jesus] asked the angel, "How will [emphasis added] this be?"

Luke 5:4–5 (MSG)
When he finished teaching, he said to Simon, "Push out into deep water and let your nets out for a catch." Simon said, "Master, we've been fishing hard all night and haven't caught even a minnow [how will]. But if you say so, I'll let out the nets."

Luke 1:18 (NIV)
Zechariah [when told that he and Elizabeth would have a child] asked the angel, "How can [emphasis added] I be sure of this?"

YEARS AGO, as I was praying, the words "may my home be a sanctuary and a safe haven" bubbled up. I wasn't sure why, or how, that would even be fulfilled, but knew if this was something the Lord wanted, He would do it. I simply said, "Lord, if You will, then I will" and every home I've lived in since has carried that covering. It's been the evacuation shelter in the middle of the night during California wildfires. It's been the sanctuary after a marriage went up in flames. It's been a peaceful retreat after a lost ID prevented the ability to fly home. It's been the in-between home for multiple women either in the process of moving or discerning where to go. No questions asked. It's always temporary but without a timeline. My "if you will, I will" gave the Lord an all-encompassing green light to bless others without my need to understand how or when or who.

Mary didn't question whether God would do what He promised. She had faith that the words spoken would happen. Similarly, Simon Peter as well as James and John (Zebedee's sons) used "how will" obedience to usher in a blessing beyond that which their boats could contain. When Jesus asked them to try again—to believe He not only could, but also would bring them fish after they'd finished working—they responded with "how will." Zechariah, on the other hand, questioned God's very identity when he asked whether He could fulfill His promise. His mouth was shut during Elizabeth's pregnancy so that the promise wouldn't be stopped or delayed by those doubting words.

A "how will" faith carries a weight to it like a heavyweight boxer getting ready to deliver knockout punches. That's the kind of faith we need in the in-between. When the weight of the wait is heavy, when we don't understand how, that's exactly when faith is pushed back into deeper water. "How can" actually says that the Lord can't. It blocks promises and breakthroughs. It's not harmless. When the world shouts "how can," we simply say one word—Jesus.

"How will" acknowledges that God can, and will, do anything. There is a real difference between the lives of those who say "how can" and those who say "how will." This world needs "how will" women who believe, with everything in us, that God will do all that He has promised. This world needs daughters who will not give up on our Father. It's time, beautiful one, to begin to say, "Lord, if You will, I will."

We lay down everything that is going on around us and all that is going on within us today. Holy Spirit, shape our thoughts, hearts, and prayers to say "how will" instead of "how can." Forgive us, Lord, for the times when our words have brought delays or detours. It may look like the work is over with no results, but this is exactly when You say to push back into the deep water. If You will, Lord, we will. We lean in with expectancy because we believe, Holy Spirit, that Your promises are true. We declare like David, Lord, show up and show out in the mighty name of Jesus! Amen.

Reflect

• • •

What does it mean to you to become a "how will" woman?

_____

_____

_____

_____

_____

What is one time that you've seen the doubt you've spoken out loud delay or deter a promise?

_____

_____

_____

_____

_____

Where do you need the Holy Spirit to guide you from "how can" to "how will" this week?

_____

_____

_____

_____

_____

Chainbreaker

• • •

Acts 16:25-26 (MSG)
Along about midnight, Paul and Silas were at prayer and singing a robust hymn to God. The other prisoners couldn't believe their ears. Then, without warning, a huge earthquake! The jail tottered, every door flew open, all the prisoners were loose.

A S I WAS PRAYING this morning, I saw a loved one with many chains. Each chain had a word on it and as I prayed, I saw the chains break off one by one. I believe God wants us to pray and destroy the chains for others that they are unable to see for themselves. As we pray over those we love, I believe that God will place on our hearts specific areas that need to be transformed in their lives. In order to live the abundant, victorious lives that we were created to live, we must come into agreement with the Lord to break every chain. I see this right now for so many in the Church who are walking in salvation, but not in victory. The Lord wants all of His children to walk in true freedom, and that can't happen when are still living like slaves.

Note that Paul and Silas were praying and singing. This was something I'd read over a hundred times and missed. How much do we do one or the other but not both? I know I am more likely to sing when I feel joyful, or when I feel that God has come through for me, and more likely to remain silent when I'm sad, or frustrated, or when I don't understand what God's doing. Here, Paul and Silas are in a prison, believing and trusting and praying and singing! Regardless of how they felt about the situation, they praised God together. Their unity in prayer and praise ushered in a powerful breakthrough. The

Lord answered in power—not just for them, but for everyone around them. Paul and Silas's faith and agreement set all of the other prisoners free!

What a tremendous privilege and responsibility it is to have the power and authority through Jesus Christ to break the chains that bind others. We have that privilege and responsibility today as followers of Christ. As the chains are broken in our own lives, and as we learn how to battle in the in-between, we're able to come alongside others and help them fight as well. Instead of one or two women rising up in victory, we become an entire army of warrior voices, bold and strong in our true identities in the Lord. We don't have to wait for this either. In fact, it can start right now, today.

Father God, I place before You, ____(name of loved one)____. I ask that You bring the blood of Your son, Jesus Christ over him/her right now. Give me eyes to see past his/her actions and discernment instead to perceive the very roots that are keeping him/her from becoming everything You desire him/her to be. Forgive me for not taking up the authority You've given me as Your daughter sooner. I am the righteousness of God in Christ Jesus, and it is my privilege and responsibility to step forward in Your Name. Reveal anything that has enabled ____(name)____ to stay chained to _____ (fear, rejection, insecurity, anger, addiction, loneliness, confusion, etc.). Forgive me, Jesus, for my part in this. Cleanse our hearts by the power of Your Holy Spirit. I now bind the spirit of _____ and lay it at the foot of the Cross, where it must burn up in the sacredness of Your Presence. I believe and declare, Lord, that You are breaking these chains right now in the mighty name of Jesus! Thank You for how You are transforming him/her at this very moment. Thank You, Jesus, for letting us be a part of __(name)'s____ healing and victory. Amen.

Reflect

. . .

When you picture a loved one with chains, who comes to mind?

_____
_____
_____
_____
_____
_____
_____
_____
_____

What are the chains on his or her life?

_____
_____
_____
_____
_____
_____
_____
_____
_____

Have you ever prayed for these chains to be broken off of his or her life? If not, why not?

_____

_____

_____

_____

_____

_____

_____

_____

_____

What would it look like to help others usher in their own breakthroughs even as you are walking out your own?

_____

_____

_____

_____

_____

_____

_____

_____

_____

_____

WEEK 24

Jericho Walls

• • •

Joshua 6:2–4 (AMP)
The Lord said to Joshua, "See, I have given Jericho into your hand, with its king and the mighty warriors. Now you shall march around the city, all the men of war circling the city once. You shall do this [once each day] for six days. Also, seven priests shall carry seven trumpets [made] of rams' horns ahead of the ark; then on the seventh day you shall march around the city seven times, and the priests shall blow the trumpets."

LAST SUMMER, the Lord woke me up at five o'clock in the morning with a vision of myself walking around a specific building seven times and declaring a breakthrough. Like a strong woman of faith, I said, "That's nice" and tried to go back to sleep. Well, there was no way that was going to happen, because when the Lord wants us to do a thing, it rises up inside of us like a fire until we obey. I got the point, got dressed, drove over, and started marching around the building. It felt a little (actually, a lot) foolish at first, but that quickly evaporated when I felt a tangible darkness and heaviness in a specific area of the building each time I circled it. That's when I realized the importance of why I was there. I started praying and declaring against that spirit until I felt it break. By the time I had gotten to the seventh time around, the Holy Spirit was filling each step with more power, to the point that it wouldn't have surprised me if concrete walls tumbled down right there! It was unlike anything I've experienced before, or since, and redefined what I thought I knew. I can now say confidently that the Holy Spirit's power rising up is more than enough to shake every foundation around or under us.

Jericho was shown and handed over to the Israelites by God before they ever took one step, but the Lord's instructions on how to take the city are completely counterintuitive. Instead of attacking, the people marched around it, in silence, once a day, for six days while the priests carried the ark of the covenant. On the seventh day, they marched around Jericho seven times with the ark of the covenant, blowing their trumpets and then shouting in victory. It's worth noting that there were seven priests blowing seven trumpets in the Book of Joshua, just as there are seven angels that sound the seven trumpets in the book of Revelation. Similar to how the Israelites take what was already theirs, in Revelation, the Lord takes back everything that's His and gives it to His people once and for all.

Here in the in-between, we'll need to pray around some things, shout at some things, and declare victory over some things before the Lord will do what only He can do. We will do things that seem counterintuitive, foolish even. But if we have the courage to obey and the wisdom to discern when it's time to stay quiet and when it's time to shout, we will watch so many Jericho Walls come down. Just like the people obeyed the Lord's instructions regardless of how bizarre it seemed, we'll be asked to do the same. We'll even need to—often—shout or declare victory before we see anything move. This is where we grasp the authority that we've been given in Christ and learn to wield our words with power from the Holy Spirit. This training ground teaches us how to usher in the areas that have already been given to us. Beautiful one, there are so many victories that are already ours!

Almighty God, You say go and we go. You say stay and we stay. You have ideas, strategies, and alignments that we could never imagine. You tore down the walls of Jericho before, and You will do it again. Thank You, Holy Spirit, that by Your power and in the name of Jesus whatever stands in the way of Your promises being fulfilled in our lives is crumbling now! Your power is mightier than the greatest wind, stronger than the fiercest storm, and yet, gentle enough to whisper to our hearts. We are just in awe, Heavenly Father, that You choose us to partner with You in this life. Thank You, Jesus, that we are walking into our Promised Land—getting ready to experience all that You've been preparing for us! Amen.

Reflect

· · ·

What walls are standing around or blocking your promises right now?

_____
_____
_____
_____
_____
_____
_____
_____

What has the Lord given over to you that you haven't taken hold of yet?

_____
_____
_____
_____
_____
_____
_____
_____

What do you need to march around—either in your mind or physically so that these walls start to fall?

_____

_____

_____

_____

_____

_____

_____

_____

What do you need to rise up and shout about—proclaiming the victory that you haven't yet seen with your eyes?

_____

_____

_____

_____

_____

_____

_____

_____

_____

_____

As If Your Life Depended on It

• • •

1 Peter 4:7–8 (MSG)

Everything in the world is about to be wrapped up, so take nothing for granted. Stay wide-awake in prayer. Most of all, love each other as if your life depended on it. Love makes up for practically anything.

1 Corinthians 14:1 (MSG)

Go after a life of love as if your life depended on it—because it does. Give yourselves to the gifts God gives you. Most of all, try to proclaim his truth.

IN MY QUIET TIME the other day, I came across 1 Peter 4:7-8. The words "as if your life depended on it" struck me. Peter used the same phrase here as Paul did in his letter to the Corinthians. Paul and Peter didn't always see eye to eye. So it got my attention that, despite their disagreements, these two agreed on this. It's such powerful language. When I think of things life depends on, I think of air, water, and food. To parallel that, prayer is how our souls breathe. Jesus is our living water, and the Word of God is the bread of life. But have we pursued lives of love as if it's the very air we breathe—the very lifeline of our existence? What does loving as if our lives depend on it even look like? If we turn to the life of Jesus, it's radical obedience, passion, sacrifice, relentless acts of service. But are we actually living any of that out today?

Love in action intentionally makes time for others, listens more, talks less, and is slow to judge. It embraces the "detours" as divine opportunities. It searches for the deeper issues of the heart instead of accepting surface level excuses. It persists in boldness while growing in gentleness, grace, and humility. It's a lot for us to improve upon, and as if that's not enough, Jesus reminds us that going after a life of love is done at all times—regardless of whether we're exhausted, hungry, overwhelmed, or even want to be around people. Regardless of whether or not others deserve it or if we feel like it, we are called to choose to pursue love. And by pursuing love, we pursue God. By pursuing love, we pursue life.

I've started reflecting on ways I've loved well and didn't love well lately. It's amazing what comes to mind! Today, the Lord reminded me that I made time not only to acknowledge but also to have real conversations with the often-ignored workers in my building. Conversely, the Holy Spirit reminded me that when I was asked to train someone who had said hurtful things to me, I declined. I withheld love from this person when the opportunity came. Now I needed the Lord to pull up the weeds of bitterness so that blooms of love could grow there. It's definitely an ongoing refining process that we can only go through with the Holy Spirit's help. How amazing will it be to become women who truly love others as if our lives depend on it! How beautiful will it be to become women who let the ripples of love become waves that crash over our lives and onto the feet of others every day.

Heavenly Father, thank You so much for giving us the truest example of what it means to pursue a life of love by sending Your son Jesus here to this world to live and die for us. Forgive us, Abba, for the ways we haven't loved well this week. Thank You for seeing how we try. Open the eyes of our hearts to see areas where we need to pursue a life of love more zealously. Give us strength in Your mighty name, Jesus, to love each other with renewed boldness. Refresh the souls that have grown weary in doing good by the power of Your Holy Spirit. Teach us how to become women who love as if our lives depend on it! We ask for a fresh outpouring of Your Holy Spirit—a fresh anointing right now. Thank You, Lord, for all You are doing that we can't yet see in the mighty name of Jesus. Amen.

Reflect

. . .

How have you loved others well this week? Where have you fallen short?

_____
_____
_____
_____
_____
_____
_____

What does it mean to you to love as if your life depends on it?

_____
_____
_____
_____
_____
_____

How different would your life look like this week if you truly lived this out?

_____
_____
_____
_____
_____

Thwarting Time

• • •

2 Chronicles 20:22 (NLT)
At the very moment they [the Israelites] began to sing and give praise, the Lord caused the armies of Ammon, Moab, and Mount Seir to start fighting among themselves.

Numbers 21:6–9 (NIV)
Then the Lord sent venomous snakes among them; they bit the people and many Israelites died. The people came to Moses and said, "We sinned when we spoke against the Lord and against you. Pray that the Lord will take the snakes away from us." So Moses prayed for the people. The Lord said to Moses, "Make a snake and put it up on a pole; anyone who is bitten can look at it and live." So Moses made a bronze snake and put it up on a pole. Then when anyone was bitten by a snake and looked at the bronze snake, they lived.

I LOVE HOW THE LORD thwarts the plans of the enemy over and over again in the Bible. That's a promise that stands true today—that the wicked will be baffled and humiliated, but the Israelites endured this as well. When the Israelites became prideful in their complaining, the Lord sent poisonous snakes that killed many of them. Afterwards, as a future sign of deep grace, He had Moses create a bronze snake that they could look upon and live. In the way they were broken, they were restored. That is what it's like when we experience a thwarting from the Lord that's covered in grace. It baffles, confuses, and humbles us from our prideful pedestals but it's done for our restoration.

As for our enemies, they are not extended the same restoration from the Lord. As we praise and sing and give glory to God in the in-between seasons, the Lord causes our enemies to fight amongst themselves. Like the Israelites, we won't even have to enter some of these battles! We will watch the Lord fight our battles and confuse the plans of the enemy. And in the moments where complaining or pride gets the best of us, the Lord will restore us fully through the blood of Jesus, our Redeemer.

Because I grew up at the beach, I have to add that a thwart is the center beam placed across the bottom of a boat. The thwart exerts pressure internally to keep the shape of the boat while preventing it from collapsing or leaking. It is the strongest part of a boat, forming a T-shaped cross. The Cross of Christ is the strongest place for us as well. If missing, our lives collapse upon themselves. As we praise our way into breakthrough, into abundance, into new life, we are growing stronger with a center support that's founded only on Him. That's the support that will keep us together in the middle of life's storms, and the one that carries the boats of our lives safely from place to place.

Father God, You are so strategic. You have plans we cannot even fathom. Thank You for allowing us to take part in Your mighty work in this world. Thank You for confusing the plans of the enemy. Thank You for protecting us—for surrounding us with Your favor as with a shield. Thank You that those who come against You, and against Your children, will not only be thwarted but also humiliated! You are our thwart, Jesus—our strongest support, and You are the One who will do the thwarting on our behalf! We praise You, Lord, that when the thwarting must be done in our own lives, You do it with such mercy—with our restoration always in sight. We believe, in the mighty name of Jesus and by the power of the Holy Spirit, that these very enemies we see today are the same ones that will collapse upon themselves tomorrow. Hallelujah! Amen.

Reflect

. . .

Where are you believing for the Lord to thwart the plans of the enemy this week? Which giants are you looking for the Lord to slay?

When have you seen the Lord step in and detour your own plans but with your restoration always in His eyes?

What does it mean to you to have Jesus as your thwart—your strongest support?

Don't Walk Away

. . .

Ruth 1:4, 8, 14 (NIV)

They married Moabite women, one named Orpah, the other Ruth . . . [After a short while on the road,] Naomi said to her two daughters-in-law, "Go back, each of you, to your mother's home" . . . At this they wept aloud again. Then Orpah kissed her mother-in-law goodbye, but Ruth clung to her.

IT'S EASY TO FORGET that the book of Ruth centers around three women. Orpah was Ruth's sister-in-law, married to Naomi's son Kilion. Ten years into their marriages, both husbands died. Widowed, the women leave their hometown of Moab for Bethlehem because the Lord was providing for His people there. Early on in the journey, Naomi tells both women to go back home to Moab and remarry, but both refuse. Naomi again tells them to turn around and finally Orpah agrees. The Bible never mentions Orpah again, but there's a lot there that applies to our lives.

They were being moved to the place of blessing.

The Lord was providing for His people in Bethlehem, not Moab. Leaving Moab was instrumental in being positioned for their blessings. The Lord had called them out of a familiar place in order to bring them into a better life. They were not meant to return to the places and the people that the Lord had already delivered them from, and neither are we. Sometimes we are in the wrong place—the wrong city, the wrong job, the wrong relationship, and we miss that the Lord repositions us to bless us.

Orpah initially said no, but then came into agreement with Naomi's doubt, grief, and despair.

She and Ruth were both strong in their no the first time. It wasn't until after Naomi laid out all the reasons why providing new husbands for them would not be possible that Orpah agreed to return to Moab. Orpah fixed her eyes on Naomi's restricted view of the situation instead of on the Lord's, and it changed the direction of her life. Just because someone else can't see the way, doesn't mean there isn't a way. Others can be blinded by their own despair, grief, or doubts. We are called to come alongside each other, but that doesn't mean coming into agreement with someone else's broken places.

There was a second covenant redeemer.
Boaz was actually one of two redeemer options for Ruth. While the closer relative declined, it struck me that there were two covenant redeemers waiting in Bethlehem for Naomi's two daughters-in-law. Had God already prepared a husband and blessing for Orpah in Bethlehem that she forfeited? We must not walk away from where the Lord is bringing us. We cannot turn back even though what's ahead is unknown and what's behind is comfortable. We must cling to the Lord as He brings us into a new level of blessing. We have no idea the goodness that the Lord has prepared for each of us. We won't come into agreement with the doubt or despair that's spoken out of another's broken places. We are women who will rise above those waves and receive everything that's been promised!

Heavenly Father, the in-between can be filled with so many ups and downs. Help Your daughters today to learn from the wisdom of the story of Orpah. Lord, may we not turn back toward anything or anyone that You have delivered us from. Cover us with the blood of Jesus so that the fear or doubt or despair of others will not be able to settle in our hearts and minds. Remind us, Holy Spirit, that just because others can't see where You're leading, doesn't mean that You aren't still leading us there. Thank You, Lord, that You have already gone ahead of us and prepared the answers and blessings for us. We don't want to miss a single thing, Jesus! Holy Spirit, take our hands and lead us forward. Don't let us walk away, in Jesus's name. Amen.

Reflect

• • •

Where have you felt the Lord repositioning you lately?

_____

_____

_____

_____

_____

_____

_____

_____

_____

How has that been, or how do you believe that will be, for your benefit?

_____

_____

_____

_____

_____

_____

_____

_____

_____

_____

What is a time when you've been tempted to come into agreement with someone else's doubt, like Orpah did with Naomi?

_____

_____

_____

_____

_____

_____

_____

_____

_____

What can you do this week to not fall into that again?

_____

_____

_____

_____

_____

_____

_____

_____

_____

_____

_____

_____

One Degree

. . .

Psalm 16:8, 11 (ESV)

I have set the Lord always before me; because he is at my right hand, I will not be shaken . . . You make known to me the path of life; in your presence there is fullness of joy; at your right hand are pleasures forevermore.

I SPENT A FEW summers at a camp in North Carolina when I was young. One of the outdoor activities that the campers competed in was archery. It was something I (surprisingly) enjoyed, but I'd often hear the counselor say, "One degree to the left" or "one degree higher." Standing far from the target, it never looked like that small adjustment would matter, and yet, it always did. In previous jobs, I traveled regularly for work and got used to hearing pilots talk about how we'd need to go several degrees off course to avoid severe weather. We'd always end up back on course, but it made the flight take longer. In a short flight, as in a short distance from an archer's bow to the target, one degree off is easy to correct. But in a longer distance, one degree can land you in an entirely different place. One degree off course in a flight from JFK to LAX, for example, takes the plane to a different state! One degree off course from a farther distance in archery takes the arrow far away from the entire target, let alone the bull's eye.

So it is with our walk with the Lord, especially in the in-between. One degree off course here may look like a shortcut, when in fact, it's a complete detour. One degree may look like a little more TV time and a little less quiet time with the Lord, or a little more time around friends who let you get lazy in your faith instead of those who sharpen you like iron. But one degree is never just one degree. One degree always starts small and ends up big. It's the difference between being intentional in our walk and drifting. It's the difference between growing in the Lord or becoming stagnant. It's the difference between a heart of flesh and a heart of stone.

We are not sprinters. The race of life is more like an Ironman Triathlon. One degree makes a big difference. So how do we stay on course? How do we not become stagnant or drift? The first way is by setting the Lord in front of us *always*. Intentionally. Every moment of every single day. The second is by training—listening to podcasts, sermons, worship music, or reading books by Christian authors. So many other things are clamoring for that spot in our minds and hearts. And, while one degree can get us off track, one degree towards the Lord can bring us to a spot better than we were even aiming for! When we focus on the Lord and remember the seriousness of how one degree can change our path, we consciously stay in the presence of the Lord. We remain in joy and peace and gratitude, which gives the Lord space to work in even greater ways in our lives. We choose, every day, whether we're moving one degree closer or away from the Lord. Choose wisely.

Almighty God, thank You for Your reminder this morning to set You, Lord, always before us. Thank You that when we do so, You promise to make known to each of us the path of life. We need You to be the compass for our hearts and minds, Holy Spirit. I pray, Lord, that You would bring to mind any areas in each of our lives where we need a course correction. Even if it's just one degree, Jesus, we know that matters and want to be on target each day. Thank You for sending the Holy Spirit to be our counselor—to whisper "one degree up" or "one degree over" into our lives. Give us ears to hear You, Lord. We pray, in the name of Jesus, that You would take our small targets, and exchange them for Your bigger ones, Your better ones, Your glorious ones. Grant us wisdom and discernment to take the right steps today that lead into the future You have planned for each of us. May we know what it truly means to be surrounded by Your pleasures forevermore. In Jesus's name I pray. Amen.

Reflect

• • •

How can you intentionally set the Lord before you this week?

_____

_____

_____

_____

_____

In what areas of your life are sensing things are off even by one degree?

_____

_____

_____

_____

_____

Where have you caught yourself drifting or stagnant, and need to course correct?

_____

_____

_____

_____

_____

_____

Where do you want your relationship with the Lord to be by this time next year?

_____

_____

_____

_____

_____

_____

_____

_____

_____

_____

Where can you grow one degree closer to the Lord this week?

_____

_____

_____

_____

_____

_____

_____

_____

_____

_____

_____

A Time for
Peace

WEEK 29

Breathe Again

• • •

Ezekiel 37:4–5, 10 (NIV)

Then he said to me, "Prophesy to these bones and say to them, 'Dry bones, hear the word of the Lord! This is what the Sovereign Lord says to these bones: I will make breath enter you, and you will come to life.'". . . So I prophesied as he commanded me, and breath entered them; they came to life and stood up on their feet—a vast army.

Malachi 4:2–3 (MSG)

"The sun of righteousness will dawn on those who honor my name, healing radiating from its wings. You will be bursting with energy, like colts frisky and frolicking. And you'll tromp on the wicked. They'll be nothing but ashes under your feet on that Day." God-of-the-Angel-Armies says so.

A FEW MONTHS BACK, I was praying with some friends at church and saw a vision of an enormous lion's head. Stretched over the Atlantic Ocean off the coast of the United States, the Lion opened His mouth and breathed across the entire land—from coast to coast. And as that happened, I saw lights of fire popping up across a map of the United States—fires that had been ignited by this fresh *ruach, or breath,* of the Lord. We have spent the last two years dealing with a virus that has attacked people's ability to breathe. It has gone around literally stealing the breath of life. I, personally, do not believe that that's a coincidence. Adam first came to life when God breathed into him. That's what set him apart from the other living creatures. Jesus breathed on his disciples when He first appeared to them after the Resurrection and told them to receive the Holy Spirit. Scripture itself is God-breathed. Breath is our literal lifeline—physically and spiritually—and it can be hard to find it in the in-between.

The in-between can bring us to a place where all we see around us are dry bones. The battle has been long. We are weary. Promises haven't come to pass yet, dreams look dead and buried, opportunities have been missed, and relationships appear past the point of reconciliation. Some things are so dead that they stink! But our God is a God of fourth-day miracles, of dry bones that live again, of buried souls that walk out of tombs alive and well. God has a never-ending supply of Spirit to breathe upon our lives once again, and He will pour out this fresh breath upon us!

It's time to start looking for evidence of the Lord's goodness. It's time to breathe in again, beautiful ones, and receive a fresh filling of the Holy Spirit. It's time to expect the Lord to act, to watch the wicked become dust under our feet, to burst with energy and become the vast army that we have been created to be! This place may look dry, dead, or like nothing good could happen, but all it takes is one move from the hand of God to change everything. All it takes is one word to bring back to life what was once gone. All it takes is one dawn to overcome the darkness. The winds of change are blowing. We have been through fiery trials, yes, but now the Lord is breathing. Refreshing is here.

Heavenly Father, You saw this moment before our lives began and orchestrated the details—large and small—that were needed to bring us to this place, at this time, during this season. Thank You, that You have made each of us unique with gifts and talents that complement each other and glorify You. We know, Holy Spirit, that You have not turned Your back on us. We need You, Jesus. We lift our hearts and stretch out our arms to You, Lord. Holy Spirit, breathe on these dry bones again. We believe, Lord, that You are resurrecting all the dreams and promises that have seemed dead in our lives. Move in our midst, Jesus. We need You. We're ready to bound out of the stalls, free and happy, and filled with the joy of the Lord that is our strength! We praise You, Almighty God, for the lives that are going to be changed forever by Your Holy Spirit. Amen.

Reflect

. . .

Where are you expecting and actively searching for the goodness of God in your life?

_____
_____
_____
_____
_____
_____
_____
_____
_____

When have you seen the Lord breathe upon the dry bones and bring them back to life again?

_____
_____
_____
_____
_____
_____
_____
_____

What or who in this season is in desperate need of a fresh breath from the Holy Spirit?

_____

_____

_____

_____

_____

_____

_____

_____

_____

Do you believe the Lord will do it? Why or why not?

_____

_____

_____

_____

_____

_____

_____

_____

_____

_____

Advent

. . .

Luke 1:20 (MSG)
"Every word I've spoken to you will come true on time—God's time."

Psalm 16:11 (ESV)
You make known to me the path of life; in your presence there is fullness of joy; at your right hand are pleasures forevermore.

I LOVE ADVENT. You know . . . the four weeks leading up to Christmas? It is, hands down, my favorite time of year. I love the way each week carries a different theme (prophecies, hope, joy, and worship). I love that it's an intentional time to refocus our hearts on the birth of Jesus and to anticipate the glory of His return. On the other hand, I'm not great at waiting. I'm the one at the grocery store that's not only counting the number of items in other people's carts, but also the number of people in each line, and the swiftness of each cashier. It's a full mathematical gymnastics session. Anyone else know what I'm talking about? There's this constant tension between the desire for the waiting season that accompanies a beautiful promise and the ability to actually . . . wait.

We know that from the virgin's womb to the empty tomb, that our God is a God of surprises, of suddenlies, and of impossibilities. But our God is also Lord of the wait. Seriously. Our God is so very much *not* in a hurry—for our benefit and His glory. At the time of Jesus's birth, it had been over 400 years since the Word of the Lord last came to the Israelites. Talk about a massive Advent season. Entire generations just waiting around for one word from the Lord—not sure when they'd ever hear from Him again! We have the hindsight of knowing that Jesus was not late, was not lost, and had not taken a detour. The Israelites didn't have that luxury. As we continue to walk through these in-between seasons, it's important to remember that. The Lord may not be early, but He hasn't taken a detour either. He hasn't forgotten, and He's not going to be late.

The in-between is an Advent of sorts. It's the wait between the promise and the fulfillment, the tension between what was and what will be. It's how we wait in this season that matters. This season can be filled with awe, peace, intentionality, or joy, just like the Advent season before Christmas. This "not yet but almost" place is the greatest time to stretch our faith. Advent literally means a "coming into being," so it's not a pointless wait. The days of wait in the in-between are actually a sign that something great is coming. Don't miss that. God created the evening before morning. There is darkness before dawn and loss before resurrection. Something great is coming! It's a vital part of our preparation because our very lives are one long Advent. We are taught in seasons of Advent because every day of our lives leads us towards the promise of being reunited with our Lord and King. Our lives are the ultimate Advent, so if we don't figure out how to do this season well, we'll be frustrated with our lives a lot of the time.

Father God, thank You for sending Your Son, Jesus, humbled as a baby, born, announced, and full of love in ways that are impossible. Thank You that miracles are normal to You. Help us to know Your complete joy and to walk closer with You today. Thank You for Your never-ending, unfailing, incredible love. May we honor the Advent of our everyday lives and wait well in this in-between season, expecting You to move mightily. Holy Spirit, remind us that You are always on time. Lord, You answer in the best ways and in the best places, and we acknowledge that there will probably be ways that are completely not what we have in mind. We want Your ways, Abba. Unfold Your glory in our lives, Jesus. Show us how we can be women who glorify You more today in the mighty name of Jesus. Amen.

Reflect

. . .

What about this in-between season, right now, has felt like one long Advent?

_____

_____

_____

_____

_____

_____

What if this was preparing you to elevate and be used by God in a new way, a different way, for His glory? How would that change your perception?

_____

_____

_____

_____

_____

What if the Advent season each year is really just training your heart for the greatest celebration to come? How would you live differently?

_____

_____

_____

_____

_____

Though . . . Yet

• • •

Habakkuk 3:17–19 (AMP)
Though the fig tree does not blossom
And there is no fruit on the vines,
Though the yield of the olive fails
And the fields produce no food,
Though the flock is cut off from the fold
And there are no cattle in the stalls,
Yet I will [choose to] rejoice in the Lord;
I will [choose to] shout in exultation in the [victorious] God of my salvation!
The Lord God is my strength [my source of courage, my invincible army];
He has made my feet [steady and sure] like hinds' feet
And makes me walk [forward with spiritual confidence] on my high places
[of challenge and responsibility].

OH, HOW MUCH we need these verses and reminders in the in-between. This is the preparation of believing the Lord above, and yes, in spite of what our eyes see. This is the test we must pass when things look completely the opposite of what the Lord has promised. It's when the Lord puts a dream in a woman's heart to be a worship leader, but she's still in the back playing the piano. Or, when a woman dreams of leading hundreds of college-aged women to the Lord, but instead keeps pouring into only a few. It's when the Lord has promised marriage, but that woman remains single for years, sometimes decades. It's the conscious choice that must be made to trust God. It's a choice that must be made every day, intentionally, until it becomes second nature in the in-between. It's the choice to rejoice. It's the choice to shout in praise when there's nothing in our lives to shout about. It's the choice to continue to believe that the Lord God is our strength no matter what our eyes see. It's the choice to have joy in all circumstances, through the Holy Spirit, even as we wait.

This is choosing to accept the shaping of our character above all else. It's the remembrance that delay is not denial. It's the reminder that our God never has and never will fail. It's aligning with the Lord in the face of all odds. At first, it feels awkward, foolish, and even painful to do. It's hard to praise the Lord for healing when doctors say it's impossible. It's painful to praise the Lord for that prodigal child who hasn't returned yet. When what we're believing for doesn't match what we see, it causes us to lay our hearts before the Lord, vulnerable and fragile, and choose that He will be our strength once more. It's saying, "I don't understand, but I choose you, Jesus." It's remembering that the Lord's words do not return void. This honor touches the heart of God. The more we speak it, the more we believe it. The more we speak it, the more we expect it. The more we speak it, the more we look for God to work, and the more the light breaks through the shadows of night.

Heavenly Father, though we are women in the wait, though what's in our hearts doesn't match what's in front of our eyes, even now, we choose to rejoice in our Lord, Redeemer, and King. We choose to praise because You are already victorious. You know the beginning from the end. You, Lord God, will not fail. You have made us steady and sure and lead us forward by the Holy Spirit with spiritual confidence as we step up to higher places of calling and responsibility. We choose You, Jesus. Over and over and over, we choose the Name above all names. The Name at which every knee will bow, and tongue will confess, "Jesus is Lord." We choose You, and we are counting on God's Rule to prevail across our lives, our nations, and our world. Amen.

Reflect

. . .

What are the promises that you're believing for but haven't seen unfold yet?

_____

_____

_____

_____

_____

Where's that area that looks like it's completely beyond repair or new life or victory? Where do you need to shout, "Yet, I will rejoice in the Lord!"?

_____

_____

_____

_____

_____

How will you remind yourself that delays are not denials, and the Lord is not finished?

_____

_____

_____

_____

_____

A Fiercely Loyal Minority

. . .

Romans 11:2–6 (MSG)

Do you remember that time Elijah was agonizing over this same Israel and cried out in prayer? "God, they murdered your prophets, They trashed your altars; I'm the only one left and now they're after me!" And do you remember God's answer? "I still have seven thousand who haven't quit, Seven thousand who are loyal to the finish." It's the same today. There's a fiercely loyal minority still—not many, perhaps, but probably more than you think. They're holding on, not because of what they think they're going to get out of it, but because they're convinced of God's grace and purpose in choosing them. If they were only thinking of their own immediate self-interest, they would have left long ago.

WE ARE SURROUNDED by things that are fake, wrapped in a culture that is desperately trying to figure out what's true. Social media, TV, movies, celebrities, airbrushed photos, fake news, and superficial conversation are just a few things that bombard our minds every day. We live in a world that tells us how to live when in actuality, that world has absolutely no idea how to live. This world runs us ragged—exhausting and isolating us. We wake up each day in a world that tells us that the church revolves around it, when in God's design (which is the actual functioning design of all life), the world revolves around the church! It's upside down and inside out.

Fortunately, we know the Truth. And we know that the Lord always has more than what we can see—just as in Elijah's day. Elijah thought he was the only one left, and there are times in the in-between when we feel this way too. But where Elijah saw only one, the Lord saw seven thousand. Where the world wants us to isolate—only seeing ourselves and what we are going through, the Lord sees thousands of his daughters going through the exact same thing.

I believe that we are women who are part of today's fiercely loyal minority—the authentic ones. Made in the image of God, but more than that; we are remade over and over daily—conforming to the Original, true Holy Spirit. Not false, but real. We are the ones holding on tight—not because of the gifts and promises that the Lord has made, although that's incredible, but because we know how much we've been saved from by His immeasurable grace. We understand the weight of our ransom payments and revere the One who paid that price.

We are women who have been chosen, redeemed, and purposed for such a time as this—and we aren't going back. We are the focus of the Lord's love. We are daughters of the King crowned with favor and honor, wearing robes of righteousness. We are alive in this season to impact the world. We are women who walk from glory to glory and strength to strength. We will not quit. We will not shrink back. We will be loyal to the finish. And there are more than we think. The world will try to tell us that we're the only ones, but that's not true. The Lord always has more people ready to fulfill His purposes. The Lord has a tribe for each of us—a community for us to pull from and pour into. He will orchestrate those divine alignments and assignments to bring us to our people until we are fiercely loyal hearts on fire, overflowing across the Earth.

Heavenly Father, deep calls unto deep. You remind us that we are part of Your loyal minority and that You have chosen us, specifically designing each of us for such a time as this. Thank You that You've placed us in this season for a reason. Thank You that the world around us needs our exact personalities, looks, gifting, style, love, sense of humor, wisdom and more.

Thank You, Holy Spirit, that we become both more authentic and more like You at the same time. May we be women whose lives tell the world how to truly live. Make us ready, Lord, to be lighthouses that influence the world for Your glory. Holy Spirit, surround and protect us with Your favor as with a shield. May Your Voice within us cut through the noises of the world around us. I thank You for all the incredible things You are doing in our lives, Abba. You are taking us from glory to glory, to the high places of blessings, handing out gifts above and below. Plant our feet in love and strengthen us for the climb as we ascend to new places, Holy Spirit. We're holding on tight, Lord, and we're not letting go! Amen.

Reflect

. . .

Where have you, like Elijah, felt like you were all alone? Allow the Lord to show you that isn't true.

_____
_____
_____
_____
_____
_____
_____
_____

What does it mean to be fiercely loyal and authentic today?

_____
_____
_____
_____
_____
_____
_____
_____
_____

How does your life reflect this?

_____

_____

_____

_____

_____

_____

_____

_____

_____

_____

What are some areas in which you could improve this week?

_____

_____

_____

_____

_____

_____

_____

_____

_____

_____

_____

_____

Hope That Endures

• • •

Romans 5:4 (ESV)
[A]nd endurance produces character, and character produces hope.

Joshua 21:45 (NIV)
Not one of the Lord's good promises to Israel failed; every one was fulfilled.

I HAVE POST-ITS with Bible verses all around my house. Verses taped to the bathroom mirror. Verses written on a card by my computer or folded into the inside cover of my journals. I've found that I'm constantly reminding myself of what God has said. And one of my main verses right now is Joshua 21:45, which reminds us that every single one of the Lord's promises will be fulfilled. It's the tether that's tied to my hope. Worldly hope is a wish, an optimistic state of mind. But biblical hope is so much more. It's the confident expectation that something good is going to happen—specifically—confidence that what the Lord has promised us will be fulfilled. The strength of this hope relies on the Lord's faithfulness, not our own. Hope is referred to as the "anchor for our souls" (Hebrews 6:19) because without it, our hearts become sick (Prov 13:12), and our souls grow weary and drift (Galatians 6:9). But did you consider how closely perseverance is tied to hope? If we can lose hope, that means we need to actively take hold of it!

Many men and women who have come before us have had to hold onto hope beyond anything that made sense. Michelangelo created over 2,000 preliminary drawings before creating the final version of the *Last Judgment*. Da Vinci worked on *The Last Supper* for over ten years. That's a decade devoted to one single painting. Thomas Edison's teachers said he was too stupid to learn anything. He then tried 1,000 times unsuccessfully to create the lightbulb. These individuals had visions, hopes, dreams, and ridiculous perseverance, just like us. They heard the same lies but kept on seeking and believing.

What if Edison had given up on attempt number 999? What if Da Vinci decided that painting *The Last Supper* was too difficult after five years? Masterpieces were birthed from the ability to endure, to persevere, and to hold tight to the hope of what could be. It's the same with our lives today. Creating a masterpiece is a process. It can be so easy to give up in the in-between, but we will be different. Our lives are becoming exquisite tapestries—each one different from the next, full of color and texture that's woven by the ultimate Artist. We are becoming women who remind ourselves that the Lord is faithful, that the promise still stands, and that none of God's words return void. Giving up is not an option. The promise will come. The words will be fulfilled. Grab ahold of that vision, hope in the Lord once more, and press on!

Almighty God, You are the anchor for our souls. You are our everlasting hope. Forgive us, Lord, for being so much like the Israelites—confident one day and ready to give up the next. Thank You for reestablishing in our minds and hearts a steadfast hope, Holy Spirit—one that does not shift or drift with the circumstances around us. Help us to grab ahold of this hope You have given and to not let go. Like Jacob wrestled with the angel of the Lord in the desert, we declare we will not let go until You bless us! May we persevere and be rewarded with the promises that You've been shaping in our lives. When we are tempted to give up, remind us that Your Word has not stopped being fulfilled in our midst. Our strength and confidence are in You, Lord, today and always. Amen.

Reflect

...

Where have you seen endurance produce character and character produce hope?

_____

_____

_____

_____

_____

_____

_____

_____

Where do you desperately need a fresh outpouring of hope that endures?

_____

_____

_____

_____

_____

_____

_____

_____

Where do you need to grab ahold of the Lord and simply not let go?

_____

_____

_____

_____

_____

_____

_____

_____

_____

_____

What's the one thing that the Holy Spirit is whispering "try once more" this week?

_____

_____

_____

_____

_____

_____

_____

_____

_____

_____

_____

_____

Grace for Today

· · ·

Exodus 16:4 (CSB)

Then the Lord said to Moses, "I am going to rain bread from heaven for you. The people are to go out each day and gather enough for that day. This way I will test them to see whether or not they will follow my instructions."

AT SOME POINT in our Christian walk, we all go through pruning seasons. The Lord will peel back everything and everyone so that all we can depend on is Him. This is a test that's meant to recreate our foundations and build us back up. But the Lord also gives us the test of provision. We forget that that is also for our preparation—to set our hearts and priorities before the Lord and follow His instructions. The Lord promises He will meet our needs in abundance each day. And yet, like the Israelites, we're so tempted to hoard it as if the Lord will not come through for us like He promised! I confess that going into this past week, I really wanted everything that I needed for the week to just pour out on Monday. I wanted to just not have to worry about anything that week, but then I realized that if I really trusted the Lord would be true to His word that week, I wouldn't be worried about how He would provide. I was ready to stuff my cheeks with grace like a chipmunk storing up for the winter, but that's just not how our God works. He cares more about our character than our comfort, and our hearts more than our hands. Like the Israelites, the Lord rains down provision for us each day. This means in order to gather it up, we must come before God daily in prayer and ask, "Lord, what do you want to tell me today? What do I need to learn or watch out for? Where are you raining down your grace, Lord? Will you show me how to follow your favor?"

Thankfully, the Lord is still true to His character—each day this week had its own measure of grace—daily different in the amount given and unique in the ways that grace was poured out. It's so tempting to want everything we need for the future in the present, and yet, the Lord says to us as He said to Moses, "I will test them in this." There is no promise for us to receive grace for all of the desperate situations that "might happen," but we are promised grace for the situations that the Lord actually brings us into. Just like the Israelites, if the Lord brings us to it, He will bring us through it. Our God provides and will not withhold the grace we need tomorrow when tomorrow comes. There will always be more than enough for every one of His children. Let's rest in this and celebrate the provision that we've been given for today. It's fresh in abundance every day and will be enough to meet our needs. As we receive this daily, we can then turn around and pour out grace upon others—meeting the needs of a broken and hurting world.

Almighty God, Your grace is sufficient, just as You promised it would be. Forgive us, Lord, for the times we've tried to grab hold of tomorrow's grace today. Thank You that You are true to Your nature, true to Your Word, and true to Your unending love for us. You are truly mighty to save, restoring and redeeming Your children a little more each day. Thank You for giving us the exact measure of grace we need for today. Teach us how to rest in that assurance so that we may be even more present for You and one another. Thank You, Holy Spirit, for the beautiful overflowing measure of grace that You're pouring out among my sisters today. Give us eyes to see what You are doing in our lives and lungs that take in deeper breaths of Your Holy Spirit. Give each of us someone today that we can point back to Your grace. May our hearts be a safe place to land for those around us. Thank You for all that You have already done and all that You are going to do, in the mighty name of Jesus. Amen.

Reflect

. . .

What measure of grace has the Lord given you this week or in this season?

_____

_____

_____

_____

_____

_____

_____

_____

_____

How has that differed from other times of your life?

_____

_____

_____

_____

_____

_____

_____

_____

_____

Where do others need to experience the Lord's grace lived out through you?

_____

_____

_____

_____

_____

_____

_____

_____

_____

_____

What can you do this week to reflect the grace that you've been given by the Lord?

_____

_____

_____

_____

_____

_____

_____

_____

_____

_____

_____

Let Peace Lead

• • •

Isaiah 26:3 (CSB)
You will keep the mind that is dependent on you in perfect peace, for it is trusting in you.

2 Thessalonians 3:16 (TPT)
Now, may the Lord Himself, the Lord of peace, pour into you his peace in every circumstance and in every possible way. The Lord's tangible presence be with you all.

RECENTLY, I WAS offered a fantastic job. Great money, benefits, and it was a role similar to one I'd been successful at previously. From the outside, it looked perfect, but I couldn't shake the feeling that something was off. After prayer, hoping to find peace, I still felt uneasy and declined it. A couple months later, the company reapproached me with the role. This time, I didn't pray or look for peace. I just assumed that because it came back around, it must be right. I was wrong. What initially felt like a bad fit, in hindsight, was me stepping out of position from the blessings that the Lord had prepared. Only God could put me back on track and He did. When He did, the first words I heard in my spirit were, "This is a breakthrough, not a punishment." It wasn't bad, but it wasn't His best. I was so relieved that God had it, had always had it, and wouldn't let the fact that I'd moved outside of the peace of His Holy Spirit ruin everything He had planned. He had an opportunity beyond what I had imagined and double what this company had offered. He had more and following His peace was the only way I'd get there.

Creating peace where there is very little takes a special touch of the Holy Spirit. I think this is one of the reasons why peace is a wonderful litmus test when it comes to knowing whether or not we are walking in God's will. There will be a lack of peace or a sense that something is "off" when it's out of sync with what the Lord wants. We know when peace is missing regarding a decision, person, or a situation. Biblical peace doesn't depend on what's happening in the world around us. It depends on what's happening within us. The Lord promises that His peace is available to us regardless of our circumstances. We are promised *shalom*—a peace that makes us whole or complete, not just calm or at rest. In true shalom, we lack nothing. Similarly, the Greek word for peace in the New Testament is *eirene*—describing unity and oneness. Biblical peace isn't just the removal of conflict, but restoration. We must go to God first—restoring peace with Him before we can experience peace within ourselves or peace with each other.

The Lord guards us and keeps us in perfect and constant peace as our minds remain steadfast on Him. As we commit ourselves to the Lord, lean on Him, and continue to hope confidently in Him, we will experience peace that surpasses all understanding. It's vital to bind up anything that has tried to steal our peace in the name of Jesus! No weapon formed against us will prosper. We are women whose faith is firm, and we will let our lives be guided by the peace that passes all understanding.

Heavenly Father, we need more of Your perfect peace at all times, and in every way. Regardless of the circumstances, we want to be overflowing with Your Holy Spirit. May peace surround us, reign supreme within us, and flow through us into the lives of those around us. We pray for peace to be our guide. Lord Jesus, in Your Holy and everlasting name, we pray that not one more day would pass where our feet are not fitted with the readiness that comes from the gospel of peace. We ask Father God, that You, the Lord of Peace, show us something new about Yourself today and how Your peace leads. We desire so much more of Your tangible presence, Lord!

Reflect

• • •

What has been stealing your peace lately?

_____
_____
_____
_____
_____
_____
_____
_____
_____

Who or what needs to be restored in your life?

_____
_____
_____
_____
_____
_____
_____
_____
_____
_____
_____

Imagine what true shalom—wholeness, completeness—would look like in your life. Where do you want to ask the Lord to bring His shalom into your mind, your heart, your life?

_____

_____

_____

_____

_____

_____

_____

_____

_____

_____

_____

What do you think would happen if you laid these things before God and asked Him to guide you by His peace once more?

_____

_____

_____

_____

_____

_____

_____

_____

_____

_____

_____

_____

Love One Another

• • •

John 13:34–35 (MSG)
"Let me give you a new command: Love one another. In the same way I loved you, you love one another. This is how everyone will recognize that you are my disciples—when they see the love you have for each other."

John 15:12-14 (AMP)
"This is My commandment, that you love and unselfishly seek the best for one another, just as I have loved you. No one has greater love [nor stronger commitment] than to lay down [one's] own life for his friends. You are my friends if you keep on doing what I command you."

EARLY ON IN MY Christian walk, I had a dream that I was with Jesus. I had the knowledge of an adult but was a small child—the size of a four- or five-year-old. While considering this mystery, I felt Jesus reach down and turn over my hand so that my palm faced up. He then took his pointer finger and began to trace in my hand the words "love one another." As I watched my palm, I realized the same words were being etched across my heart—almost like a tattoo. It wasn't just enough for the words to be traced on me, they had to be inscribed within me. I didn't understand what was happening, but I knew that I'd never be the same. Even now, years later, sometimes when I worship, I close my eyes and place my hand on my heart and feel those words come alive again.

The way we love is supposed to be our very identity, but wow, how we've fallen short of this in the Body of Christ. Loving others the way Jesus loves us is how we show the world who we are and Whose we are. "In the same way

I loved you" means selflessly, sacrificially, patiently, with kindness and honor, loving those around us. Yes, this includes those who don't deserve our love. We didn't deserve the love of Jesus. It's not about deserving. It means blessing as many people as we can, in as many ways as we can, for as long as we can. It's about a story and purpose larger than our individual lives.

One of the ways that the Lord has stretched me during the in-between is by asking me to bless others anonymously. We're called to bless friends, strangers, and even enemies—in big ways and small ways, while we're still waiting for our own answered prayers. It's how we grow. It was difficult and awkward at first, but you know what? This has transformed me. It's so exciting now and I love it. Usually both the person and the blessing seem completely random. And yet, it ends up being something amazing. Every single time. It's a sacred thing to partner with the Lord in bringing His Kingdom from heaven to earth, so let's be women who rise to the challenge, say yes to the beautiful, tough things and pass the test.

Lord, we are so sorry. We have not loved others as You have loved us. Forgive us, Jesus, for the times when we have loved others based upon how well they've loved us first. We cannot love anyone well, ourselves included, without You, Holy Spirit. We need You so much. Please show us how to love one another—how to really walk this out. Thank You for giving us opportunities to shine Your light and Your truth into the hearts of those around us. Show us who we can bless this week. Place the people and situations on our hearts that are on Yours right now, in Jesus's name, Amen.

Reflect

. . .

Do you love others when it's inconvenient? When others look at you, how do they sense the love of the Heavenly Father?

_____

_____

_____

_____

_____

_____

_____

_____

Are you really at home in the love of Jesus, or do you just visit from time to time?

_____

_____

_____

_____

_____

_____

_____

What if those that are most difficult for you to love have been placed in your life specifically so that you can help them see that Jesus is real?

_____

_____

_____

_____

_____

_____

_____

_____

_____

_____

_____

_____

Who can you start blessing anonymously this week?

_____

_____

_____

_____

_____

_____

_____

_____

Humility

. . .

Jeremiah 32:27 (NIV)
"I am the LORD, the God of all mankind. Is anything too hard for me?"

RECENTLY DID a software update on my car and, somehow, some of the technology just stopped working. At first, it was nice being disconnected, but since it's easy to spend a ton of time driving in Los Angeles, that didn't last. Determined to fix this, I read the tech integration section of the owner's manual, watched YouTube DIY videos, and did multiple Google searches. Each time, everything would start to work, my hope would rise, and then just . . . nothing. Over and over. The more I tried, the worse it got!

Finally, I gave in and went to the dealership. This simply had to be the result of some massive software glitch. The technician got in my car, pressed a couple buttons, and had the entire thing working in under three minutes! I was both horrified and thankful. I couldn't understand why it hadn't worked for me, but, when the tech got his hands on the car, it all worked perfectly. Driving away, I felt the Lord say to me, "If a human expert can fix things quickly, how much more can I?" Ugh. I'll take humility with a side of conviction for one. Here I was, struggling in my own strength, spinning in mental circles, wasting time, when the answer was a simple, immediate fix for the expert.

As the Lord's creation, He is the expert of our lives. He fixed the very first problem (that of man being alone) with the creation of Eve. She was the world's first answer. As women, we echo Eve. We hold within us solutions that the Lord wants to bring forth into the world. But we have to be humble enough to ask for help. This is such an important lesson of the in-between.

The Lord really does have answers that we cannot see and assignments that are divinely prepared. The Lord has a higher view of everything that's going on around us and within us right now. We are only given pieces, not the entire picture. As frustrating as this can feel, it's meant to remind us that God is God, and we are not. We need the Lord for everything—large and small. Our "fixing" is really just interfering. It delays the blessings because it draws our eyes off of the Lord as our Provider.

Until we learn that, we simply cannot step out of the in-between. We'll keep circling the mountain. And that's not a punishment. It's a protection. The Promised Land, with all of its goodness and abundance, would crush us if we weren't living each day humbly, holding our blessings loosely—with a constant awareness of Who is truly in control. The magnitude of the ministry that's meant to come out of the mess will crush us if we aren't matured. And we don't get to decide when we're ready. God does. It's about learning that the Lord is always right, not focusing on whether or not we are wrong.

Heavenly Father, I thank You for using the ordinary to teach us about the extraordinary. Thank You, Lord, for reminding us that nothing is too hard for You or too small. Keep us alert for what You want to do next. Keep refining our character. Soften our hearts, Holy Spirit, so that we may be humble followers of Your awesome majesty. We believe that we won't be able to round up enough containers to hold everything that You are generously pouring out into our lives. Don't let us keep circling this mountain, Lord. Help us to learn this lesson once and for all. We are so grateful for the specific, individualized moments that You have handcrafted out of Your immeasurable love for us. Give us a special sensitivity to these things in the mighty name of Jesus. Amen.

Reflect

. . .

Would you consider yourself a humble woman? Why or why not?

_____

_____

_____

_____

_____

_____

_____

_____

_____

Where are you circling some mountains in this in-between season?

_____

_____

_____

_____

_____

_____

_____

_____

_____

_____

_____

Where is the life you're living a reflection of the Lord being in control?

_____
_____
_____
_____
_____
_____
_____
_____
_____
_____

Where do you think you could grow in humility?

_____
_____
_____
_____
_____
_____
_____
_____
_____
_____

How the Lilies Grow

• • •

Matthew 6:28–29 (NRSV)
"And why do you worry about clothing? Consider the lilies of the field, how they grow; they neither toil nor spin, yet I tell you, even Solomon in all his glory was not clothed like one of these."

PLANTS HAVE NEVER been my thing, so I didn't think much about how lilies grow until recently. Associated with devotion, purity, and love, lilies were abundant in Galilee. They bloom three out of four seasons of the year and are abundant on the hills and mountains where Jesus gave His sermons, so it makes sense that He referred to them. Lilies have a natural elegance and grow without any protective thorns. They lack the outer protective layer that other flowers have, so they must be planted carefully in soil that has already been broken up. They also need to be about six-to-eight inches apart from other bulbs because they expand so much. Because they are planted deep, it appears as if no growth is happening for months, and then all of a sudden, stems shoot up and blossom. They can grow to six feet tall—stretching and leaning towards the sun. When pruned no more than one-third of their growth, they only multiply further.

Like lilies, we are completely dependent on God for our protection. Our faith must be planted deep in the good soil of our hearts that has already been broken up. We are made to flourish, and as such, can't grow in shallow ground. The deeper our lives are planted in the Lord, the stronger our roots and the higher we will grow. We will all spend an entire season (or multiple seasons) of growth in the dark. This is one of the benchmarks of the in-between.

Like a good gardener, the Lord examines how we're growing in the dark. Only, it'll be watching what we do when it feels like we're being overlooked. Or, like the hardened outer core of a seed cracking open in the dark, how we react when others get their breakthroughs, their promises, or their dreams fulfilled before us. It's right there that the Lord will teach us to be genuinely and truly happy for the growth of others so that we can receive our own well. We have not been overlooked or dismissed with a heavy hand. We have been hidden with tremendous care and gentleness. This is a protected place. A place that's just between us and God. The Lord does some of His best and deepest growth in our lives when it looks like absolutely nothing is happening on the surface. Even when we are pruned, it's a set amount at a set time and always so that we can grow far beyond where we are. The hidden work strengthens us, while the pruning lets us know that we're about to launch forward! Just because this is hard, doesn't mean it isn't good.

Once we let the Lord complete that process, we grow quickly. When it's time, the Lord will shoot us forth and expand our capacity. Like lilies stretching towards the sun, we reach towards the light of Jesus in this place. Like lilies receiving the rain, the Lord provides blessings that we simply receive. Lilies are beautiful without having to show off too. We, beautiful ones, will exude a natural elegance and fragrance as we become beautiful with the fragrance of Christ without even realizing it!

Heavenly Father, thank You for telling us to consider the lilies. There is so much wisdom packed into this simple flower, and it's easy to overlook all that You have for us to learn here. Thank You, Jesus, that every word You gave us is for our benefit. May we, as daughters, wives, mothers, and sisters in Christ, flourish like lilies this year. Plant us in good soil with hearts deeply rooted in You. May we stretch and soak in the Son—receiving everything that You have for us. Resting in the assurance that You, Almighty God, are taking good care of us. Help us, Holy Spirit, to remember that we are the pleasing aroma of Christ among those who are being saved. Amen.

Reflect

· · ·

What about lilies jumps out most to you this week?

_____
_____
_____
_____
_____
_____
_____
_____
_____
_____

Where does this parallel your own life in this season?

_____
_____
_____
_____
_____
_____
_____
_____
_____
_____

What about the in-between has been a protected place for you?

_____

_____

_____

_____

_____

_____

_____

_____

_____

What do you need to simply receive from the Lord today?

_____

_____

_____

_____

_____

_____

_____

_____

_____

_____

_____

Double

· · ·

Job 42:10 (NRSV)
And the Lord restored the fortunes of Job when he had prayed for his friends; and the Lord gave Job twice as much as he had before.

Isaiah 61:7 (NIV)
Instead of your shame you will receive a double portion, and instead of disgrace you will rejoice in your inheritance. And so you will inherit a double portion in your land and everlasting joy will be yours.

BOTH OF THESE verses speak about a double portion provided by the Lord. The first in response to Job interceding for others, and the second a future promise for the Israelites. It was Job's prayers for his friends that was the catalyst for his own double portion. It was the Lord's promise through Isaiah that gave the Israelites hope for the future. I love that as Jesus began His ministry, Isaiah 61 was the first Old Testament section that He quoted to the people in His hometown of Nazareth. With so many amazing nuggets of truth, hope, and promise in Scripture, choosing this reminder of God's double blessing and everlasting joy is significant.

I had a conversation with a friend recently who has been struggling with some professional changes. At the outset, these changes had the potential to be negative because it involved repositioning friends and potentially a physical relocation. But I found myself saying, "What if God really is as good as He says He is? What if this is enlarging your tent, not pruning you? What if this is the beginning of a brand-new blessing?"

I thought about that. What if Jesus was speaking these verses to us today? Have we truly interceded for the doubters? The people in our lives who are difficult? What if we knew that we would receive a double portion for everything we've been through? What if everlasting joy really is ours? What if there really is a great inheritance coming to each of us that will cause us to rejoice like never before? What if God is not only restoring what was lost but also giving each of us more than before?

The in-between is the best place to start answering those questions. It's a place that prepares us to step out in a whole new level of faith and expectancy in who God is and what He will do. Like Job, are we praying for our friends? I hope we are interceding for others and believing in a double portion of blessings. I hope we are stretching our faith for more in this season. Let's start living as if *all* of Who God is and what He promises is true.

Holy, Heavenly Father, You speak truth because You are truth. You are everlasting joy and life abundant. You are where love begins. Everything You have for us is good. Every word, every promise, every dream that You place in our hearts. You have so much more for us, Lord. Get us out of our own way, so that You can flow through us mightily. Jesus, we love You. Holy Spirit, may we take steps of faith knowing that Your promises are unfolding in our lives. I pray that You would give each woman reading this an expectant mind and heart to see You work! Thank You, Abba, that You don't repay with a little, or just enough, but instead with a double portion. Thank You, Lord, that You are the God of more than enough. Show up and show off in our lives, Lord. Leave us in awe and wonder of You, in Jesus's name. Amen.

Reflect

• • •

How are you living as if you really believe the Lord is restoring what was lost in your life?

_____

_____

_____

_____

_____

Are you living and believing that you are the daughter of a King with a royal inheritance? Why or why not?

_____

_____

_____

_____

Where are you believing for and due for a double blessing?

_____

_____

_____

_____

_____

This Salty Life

• • •

Matthew 5:13 (AMP)

"You are the salt of the earth; but if the salt has lost its taste (purpose), how can it be made salty? It is no longer good for anything, but to be thrown out and walked on by people [when the walkways are wet and slippery]."

GROWING UP AT the beach, the phrase "Salt Life" referred only to a surfing apparel company. It's a reference to life on the water. Men and women who love the beach, the waves, ocean wildlife, surfing, paddle boarding, deep sea fishing, and sailing. It's also the life we are called to live as Christians. Bringing others into the oceans of mercy, grace, and love that we adore. Jesus tells us that we, as Christians, are the salt of the earth, but how do we really live this salt life?

Salt can be used for seasoning food, to toss on ice to dry it out, or more commonly in Jesus's day, as a preservative. A little bit of salt is great for seasoning meat, but too much and that same food turns into something horrible that cannot possibly be swallowed. Too much of a good thing quickly becomes a bad thing where salt is concerned. Similarly, we are the seasoning of life to a world that can otherwise taste pretty awful. It only takes a little bit of our love for God to get the attention of an unbelieving world. Too much at the wrong time or in the wrong way has the opposite effect. It can end up pushing away from Jesus the very people that we were trying to draw closer to Him. This is similar to taking in too much salt and hardening our arteries. Asking unbelievers to take in more than they are currently built to handle. We can lead others to Jesus, but their faith must be their own. I think back to my own walk with the Lord and remember how, in college, I didn't want to be friends with the kids who were "too Christian." Trying to force it just pushed me away from the Lord more.

On the rare occasion that it snowed in my hometown growing up, it always turned into ice, so we'd have bags of salt ready to go for steps, sidewalks, driveways, and parking lots. Dumping salt breaks down the composition of the ice so that roads or steps can be accessed safely. This "faith dumping" is awesome within the Christian community and powerful when dealing with the lies, attacks, or spirits of the enemy. Dumping the truth of Christ on top of the attacks that come against us breaks them down the same way that the salt breaks down the ice. Pouring out our testimonies also helps break down barriers for others and allows them to walk forward into their own healing or breakthrough. As Christians, we are here, on purpose, to point others to Jesus—literally preserving them and ourselves. And we don't need a little seasoning of faith to do that—we need a lot of faith, all the time, every day, to enable us to continuously be the saltiness, the flavor of life within this world.

Heavenly Father, You made the oceans full of salt, teeming with life, and then called us to be salt of the world. Holy Spirit, give us wise and discerning hearts. Help us to sprinkle where we need to be seasoning and to dump where we need to break some things down. Above all, Lord, help us all to be faith-filled women who preserve the ones we love. Give us enough faith to stand in the gap and fight for one another, encouragement to build each other up, and wisdom to know the best use of our faith in each circumstance that we encounter. Lord, may our lives exude seasoning. May the stories, plans, and purposes You have for each of us draw others closer to You so that they also may improve the world around us. Amen.

Reflect

. . .

Where are you sprinkling your faith where you need to be dumping it and vice versa?

_____

_____

_____

_____

_____

_____

_____

_____

Where would you say that your faith, lived out loud, has helped preserve others?

_____

_____

_____

_____

_____

_____

_____

_____

Where are you surrounding yourself with those whose faith helps preserve you?

_____

_____

_____

_____

_____

_____

_____

_____

_____

How are you using words of faith, words of truth, and your testimony to break down the barriers, lies, or attacks that come against those you love?

_____

_____

_____

_____

_____

_____

_____

_____

_____

Gratitude

. . .

Luke 17:15–19 (NIV)

One of them, when he saw he was healed, came back, praising God in a loud voice. He threw himself at Jesus' feet and thanked him—and he was a Samaritan. Jesus asked, "Were not all ten cleansed? Where are the other nine? Has no one returned to give praise to God except this foreigner?" Then he said to him, "Rise and go; your faith has made you well."

Luke 7:38, 47 (NIV)

As she stood behind him at his feet weeping, she began to wet his feet with her tears. Then she wiped them with her hair, kissed them and poured perfume on them . . . "Therefore, I tell you, her many sins have been forgiven—as her great love has shown. But whoever has been forgiven little loves little."

I'M IN THE BOOK of Leviticus right now and realized that Jesus's instruction to the lepers to show themselves to the priests was exactly what they were supposed to do according to their customs and religious laws. This was what they had been doing for centuries! And though all ten lepers were cleansed, only one leper was made well and recognized for having faith. Some translations say he was "made whole." This means that, in Jesus's eyes, being cleansed and being made well are entirely different things. For the one who returned, praising loudly, gratitude had driven out pride.

Realizing this brought to mind the story of the woman who washed the feet of Jesus with her tears. She had been forgiven of much and brought her sacrifice of praise and her tears of gratitude to the feet of Jesus. She placed the only things she had of value: her hair and her perfume, on the dirty feet of Jesus. She knew He was the One who had made her well. Gratitude had driven out fear.

The Bible doesn't elaborate on the lives of these two before meeting Jesus, but they were both outcasts in society. They both understood the magnitude of what Jesus had done for them and were open, vulnerable, and deeply grateful. They showed it in different ways: one praised loudly, while the other cried, but their hearts were still the same. May we be like them. It's through gratitude—whether that be falling at the feet of Jesus or praising God for what He's doing that we are made whole. When we really know the depth of how the Lord has not only cleansed us, but also made us well, we are never the same. We never stop being thankful. We don't want to stop praising or pouring out all that was once important to us upon the feet of Jesus.

We become women who are known by our great love, because we are women who have experienced *the* great love. Gratitude—in the big and the small things—opens the windows of heaven. The Lord wants to bless us. It's time to not only thank Him for what He's done in the past, but also for all we're believing for Him to do in the future. I don't know who the other nine lepers thanked, if anyone, but Jesus had more for them, and they missed out. Being cleansed was a miracle but it wasn't the whole miracle. Withholding our thanks may cause us to miss out on the more that the Lord wants to do!

Almighty God, show us where You are doing the extraordinary in the middle of the ordinary. We want to be like those who came back praising (loudly!) or falling at the feet of Jesus in utter amazement. Create in us hearts and mouths that are quick to thank You, Lord. You are always more ready to give than we are to receive, Lord. Thank You, Holy Spirit, that gratitude and fear, gratitude and anger, and gratitude and pride cannot coexist. Thank You for designing the world this way. Every single good thing we have comes from You. It's more than we deserve or understand, but we praise You, Jesus. Amen.

Reflect

. . .

When has the Lord told you to do something that seemed ordinary but had a radically different outcome?

_____

_____

_____

_____

_____

_____

Where do you identify with the one leper who comes back to thank Jesus? Where do you identify with the other nine lepers who kept going about their days?

_____

_____

_____

_____

_____

Where do you see yourself cleansed but not whole?

_____

_____

_____

_____

_____

_____

Unshakeable and Trustworthy

• • •

Psalm 16:8 (NIV)
I keep my eyes always on the Lord. With him at my right hand, I will not be shaken.

Psalm 139:23–24 (NRSV)
Search me, O God, and know my heart; test me and know my thoughts. See if there is any wicked way in me, and lead me in the way everlasting.

WHEN I FIRST became a Christian, I asked the Lord for two things: to make me a woman of unshakeable faith and to make me a woman who He could trust. I'm so thankful now that I had no idea what I was actually asking for when I prayed that prayer. If I had known, I'm not sure I would've been able to pray that. I didn't even know what it meant to be a woman of unshakeable faith or a woman who the Lord could trust; let alone the processes involved to get there. All I knew was that, in the deep places of my heart, that's who I wanted to be.

We don't become women of unshakeable faith without being shaken. A lot. We don't become women that the Lord deems trustworthy without being tested. A lot. So, my prayer was essentially asking the Lord to shake me and test me until everything that wasn't of Him had fallen away. The deepest desire of my heart had become Psalm 139. In order to become unshakeable, I had to learn Who would keep me from being shaken. I had to relearn my identity in Christ, and along with it, find the Rock upon which I'd rebuild my life. In order to become a woman who God could trust, I had to let the Lord hammer away the hardened places, the fortresses built out of fear, or rebellion, or bitterness and let the Lord truly exchange a heart of flesh for that heart of stone. And, I had to let the Lord do that work many, many times over. I had to decide, once and for all, that I would not come out of this the same way I went into it. I had to decide that I had not come this far to only come this far.

Don't waste this in-between season, beautiful one. This is a place to claim victory over all the lies of the enemy and the pain of the past. This is a place to be made new. This is the place to be shaken in the safe embrace of the One who laid down His life for us. This is the place to let our tests become our testimonies. This is the time to let those chains fall off once and for all. This is a season to be transformed from the inside out so that all the world can see exactly how good and how mighty the Lord truly is.

This is the dance of the overcomer! All of the sifting and stirring—it's emotional, hard, and exhausting—but the beauty that pours out of it will drive us to our knees in thankfulness. This is the pressing that makes the best wine. We will rise up, realizing our hearts have become knit with the heart of God in ways we never thought possible. The depth of our loss will become the depth of our love. The pain will suddenly have a purpose. The years the locusts have stolen will begin to be repaid. The attacks of the enemy will be drowned out by the voice of Truth. We will cry tears of joy at how great our God really is and the heights of His love for us. We will know that our God is pleased with us as we're propelled into the new. Our praises will leap before us, bounding over ground that springs up with the goodness of God. Our victories begin right here, right now in the in-between.

Almighty God, we want to be women who are of unshakeable faith that You can trust. Examine our hearts and minds, Lord, and do whatever You need to do to change us. As scary as it is to pray that prayer, Holy Spirit, we know that You are good, and You only have good for us. Continue the incredible work that You have begun in us. Please don't let us come out of this season the same way we went into it. Amen.

Reflect

. . .

How do you want to be different as you walk through this in-between season?

_____

_____

_____

_____

_____

_____

What, specifically, do you want the Lord to transform in your heart? Your life?

_____

_____

_____

_____

_____

Where can your praises go before you this week?

_____

_____

_____

_____

_____

A Time to
Laugh, A Time
to Dance

WEEK 43

The Power of Laughter

. . .

Job 5:22 (AMP)
You will laugh at violence and famine, [a]nd you will not be afraid of the wild beasts of the earth.

Proverbs 31:25 (NIV)
She is clothed with strength and dignity; she can laugh at the days to come.

Psalm 126:2 (NRSV)
Then our mouth was filled with laughter, and our tongue with shouts of joy; then it was said among the nations, "The Lord has done great things for them."

DOES IT FEEL impossible to laugh right now? It might sound ridiculous to think about this, but there has been, and continues to be, *a lot* positioned to attack our joy. Thankfully, the Bible says that we can and will laugh at the days to come. This means we can laugh in the face of all that is unknown. We can still find joy in the midst of sickness, political unrest, legal battles, financial insecurity, job uncertainty, family, and relationship difficulties. Laughter reminds our souls that the joy of the Lord is our strength.

Laughter defeats the spirit of heaviness. Laughter in the face of adversity takes our minds off our own inabilities and focuses on God's abilities. We have a God that goes before us to fight our battles. We have a God that has put power in laughter—to heal minds, bodies, and souls. God Himself laughs at our enemies before He unleashes His wrath upon them, according to Psalm 2:4, "[b]ut the One who rules in heaven laughs," and Psalm 37:13, "but the

Lord laughs at the wicked, for He sees that their day is coming." When we laugh in the spirit, we remind ourselves that God is setting all things right and that the enemy will *not* win. We laugh because we know the end of the story and where the victory has always, and will always, remain.

As the world grows darker, we need the Holy Spirit to show us where the Lord is laughing. We need to see things from a higher perspective so that we can hold our joy, and therefore our strength, in the midst of increasing difficulty. We are women of Proverbs 31—laughing at the days to come. We are not afraid of the future because we rest in the One who holds it in His hands. We are women who are walking out lives that will cause others to say, "The Lord has done great things for them!" We are women who will have reason to rejoice. We will not look at all that is around us but will instead look upon the One who surrounds all that surrounds us. We will let the Holy Spirit stir joy up in our hearts once more. We can and will keep the joy of the Lord as our strength while on our way to victory because we are confident in the One who goes before us!

Heavenly Father, we know that You are laughing at our enemies right now at this very moment. You are not intimidated by what You see on this earth. You laugh because You have already seen the plans of the enemy destroyed. Help us to remember that we, too, walk in Your victory, Jesus. May we, our families, our relationships, our work, and our homes be filled with laughter and the joy of the Lord regardless of the circumstances around us.

Show us, Holy Spirit, things that we can laugh about when life leaves our emotions and hearts dry. Fill our hearts with joy as we watch Your victorious plans unfold upon the earth. May those who You have placed in our spheres of influence lift their eyes to You and say, "Look what amazing things the Lord has done for them." Amen.

Reflect

• • •

Where do you need the Lord to stir up your joy today?

_____

_____

_____

_____

_____

_____

_____

_____

_____

Where do you want to become a woman who laughs at the days to come?

_____

_____

_____

_____

_____

_____

_____

_____

_____

What about this season has made laughing feel impossible?

_____
_____
_____
_____
_____
_____
_____
_____
_____
_____

What is one thing each day that you will laugh about this week?

_____
_____
_____
_____
_____
_____
_____
_____
_____
_____
_____

Radiant

. . .

Luke 8:16 (ESV)
"No one after lighting a lamp covers it with a jar or puts it under a bed, but puts it on a stand, so that those who enter may see the light."

Isaiah 60:1 (AMP)
"Arise [from spiritual depression to a new life], shine [be radiant with the glory and brilliance of the Lord]; for your light has come, And the glory and brilliance of the Lord has risen upon you."

THE LORD GAVE me a vision while I was hiking the other day. I saw a candle that was lit but the flame was small, not giving off much heat or light. The candle was in a wooden box that was solid on three sides with a wooden top and bottom. The fourth and front side had iron bars on the top part of it with open spaces between them, similar to an old jail cell. Suddenly, a gust of air came in through the open spaces in between the bars and instead of blowing out the light, it ignited it more! The flame was suddenly higher and hotter—to the point at which it burned down the wooden case around it and completely melted the iron bars. How does light forget it's light? A candle doesn't forget to burn, but it's not radiating light or heat or power when there's a tiny flame. It's designed for more.

When we're in the in-between, when the process of preparation has been longer and harder than we ever imagined, we can forget what we were created for. We begin to believe that beauty is in the eye of the beholder, but that's not true. Beauty is in the eye of the Creator. He decides what is beautiful and what isn't. Beautiful ones, as women, we were created to be radiant. We are lights created to be set on fire. We are flames designed to burn down the darkness. According to *Merriam-Webster,* radiant means "to shine or glow brightly, glowing, marked by an expression of love, confidence, or happiness." Radiance is so special because it's all about what's inside of us, coming out of us, to change what's around us. The more we look to Jesus, the more radiant we become. Then others look to us and see that glory and brilliance of the Lord shining through us. A radiant face doesn't have shadows of fear, doubt, or worry across it. Eyes that are radiant reflect a heart that is pure and sure. The in-between wasn't created to imprison us or to shut away the light. It's time to let the Holy Spirit breathe on us again. It's time for bars of iron to melt and walls to crumble from the heat of the flame.

The radiance of the Lord pours light into a world that is increasingly dark. Our creativity is needed. Our gentleness is needed. Our laughter is needed. Our gifts are needed. Our anointing is needed. Our love is deeply, deeply needed. We must remind ourselves that we really are lights on a hill, waves of joy bubbling up and crashing over weary hearts in a land that has been dark for far too long. We were created to shine and stand out, not fade against the darkness. We are covenant bearers and glory carriers. We are women of promise, purpose, praise, and prayer. We are meant for more and we won't stop until we're there. Fan the flame and let it burn like never before!

Holy Spirit, fill us afresh with Your anointing and presence. Your commands are radiant and obeying them makes us shine like we never could on our own. Thank You, Heavenly Father, that as we look to You, You make us increasingly radiant in ways we could never comprehend. Transform us, so that we may be lights strategically positioned along the way for others. May our lives point them to You. Radiate joy, peace, confidence, love, hope, mercy, grace, goodness, kindness, and patience to those who need it the most. Thank You, Jesus, that You make us mirrors of Your splendor as You take us from glory to glory. Set our hearts on fire, Lord, as You burn down the bars of iron in our lives and lift our faces to You. Amen.

Reflect

• • •

What if you lived each day this week completely unafraid to shine?

_____
_____
_____
_____
_____
_____
_____
_____
_____

How would this change the face of the earth?

_____
_____
_____
_____
_____
_____
_____
_____
_____

How different would we be if each day we walked in step with the glory of the Lord moving across our lives?

_____

_____

_____

_____

_____

_____

_____

_____

_____

_____

What's one thing you can do this week to remember that you are a flame created to burn?

_____

_____

_____

_____

_____

_____

_____

_____

_____

_____

_____

Rahab's Redemption

· · ·

Joshua 2:11b–12 (NIV)
"[F]or the Lord your God is God in heaven above and on the earth below. Now then, please swear to me by the Lord that you will show kindness to my family, because I have shown kindness to you. Give me a sure sign."

Joshua 6:17 (ESV)
And the city and all that is within it shall be devoted to the Lord for destruction. Only Rahab the prostitute and all who are with her in her house shall live, because she hid the messengers whom we sent.

RAHAB WAS courageous—hiding the Israelite spies and lying to the King's men to protect them. She created a covenant with the people who were her enemies by boldly asking for a sign of kindness, and protection for her family. She exhibited great discernment, knowing that the God of the Israelites is the One True God. She was positioned well and "happened" to live in Jericho, the city blocking the Israelites' entrance to the Promised Land. She was a prostitute, so no one would second guess strange men entering her home, and she "happened" to live in a house that backed up to the city wall.

Rahab was all these things before she was saved. But afterward, she was given so much more. She was provided with a new identity. Rahab was initially introduced as "a prostitute named Rahab"—known by her deeds first and by name second. But after this, every other reference in the Bible calls her "Rahab the prostitute." She experienced mercy, safety, and rescue. It never says that anyone else in Rahab's family believed in the Lord, and yet, they were all saved because of her. Joshua 6:23 makes a point of noting that her father and mother and brothers were brought out of Jericho by the Israelites.

She was unmarried, her parents were still alive, and she had brothers to take the lead in covering, protecting, and providing for her. The Lord flips this upside down and uses her to provide and protect all of them! She's given abundant provision. Rahab (and her whole family) are given a free place to live by the Israelites. Not only was she saved by the very people that were considered her enemies, but also they then gave her land for her family to live on. She was the one in her family that the Lord used to bring breakthroughs and usher in generational blessings. Rahab was a Canaanite in Jericho and should have perished with the rest of the city, ending her family line. But God had other plans.

In divine redemption, Rahab married a man from the tribe of Judah (an Israelite)—a covenant marriage to redeem her former life as a prostitute and became the mother of Boaz, which makes her great-great-grandmother to King David. We know from the story of Ruth that Boaz was quite wealthy, so she also had financial provision along with land to pass on to her descendants. She also is in the lineage of Jesus—reminding us that absolutely nothing is outside the boundaries of the Lord's grand plan of redemption.

Heavenly Father, thank You so much for the story of Rahab. Thank You for the many ways that You not only redeemed her but also her entire family and future! There is so much for us to learn about all of the incredible ways that You choose to redeem our lives just in these passages of Joshua alone. Our lives are one large mosaic of redemption. Thank You for Your Word—the clarity it brings, the power, revelation, and encouragement it brings. Thank You, Holy Spirit, that You work where there seems to be no way. Thank You, Jesus, that this story of redemption is a glimmer of all that You have sacrificed to give us. Bless my sisters here, Abba. Surround them with Your favor as with a shield. May these words of redemption ignite a fire in their hearts and speak into all the spaces of their lives. We love You with all of our hearts, souls, and minds, Holy Spirit, and embrace with eagerness all of the redemption You are doing in us and through us. In Jesus's name. Amen!

Reflect

. . .

If the Lord can do all of this for Rahab, how much more can He do for you?

_____

_____

_____

_____

_____

_____

Where could the Lord use you to be the one to change the script for your entire family and generations to come?

_____

_____

_____

_____

_____

Where do you need to start building faith for a Rahab-style redemption?

_____

_____

_____

_____

_____

_____

Flourish

. . .

Isaiah 54:17 (AMP)

"No weapon that is formed against you will succeed; [a]nd every tongue that rises against you in judgment you will condemn. This [peace, righteousness, security, and triumph over opposition] is the heritage of the servants of the Lord, [a]nd this is their vindication from Me," says the Lord.

1 John 4:4 (NLT)

But you belong to God, my dear children. You have already won a victory over those people, because the Spirit who lives in you is greater than the spirit who lives in the world.

Hebrews 10:39 (ESV)

But we are not of those who shrink back and are destroyed, but of those who have faith and preserve their souls.

IN THE IN-BETWEEN seasons, it's easy to feel like it's two steps forward, one step back half the time. Or all of the time. We obey the Lord and things turn out differently than we thought they would. Or we clearly see God's hand of victory over one area of life but not another. The Lord has promised us victory in Him and through Him. His victory is our victory. He has declared we already have it, and yet, it's still a fight. And it was smack in the middle of one of these "Why have You come through for me in this area but not that area?" self-pity moments that I felt the Holy Spirit whisper, "Flourish here." How was I supposed to flourish in the middle of the battle? Could I believe that the areas of my greatest fights were also the areas of my greatest promise?

The Hebrew word for flourish is *parach*, meaning to revive, blossom; become apparent; prosper; spread out/enlarge; shoot/sprout or break forth. Flourishing is less about becoming something different than it is about breathing back to life (reviving) who and what we were originally created to be. And as we grow in Christ with our identities replanted in Him, we pierce the battle lines of the enemy. There will be weapons that come against us, but *they will not prosper (flourish)*. There have been, and will be, hurtful words spoken, or actions taken, but because we belong to God, those attacks will fall flat. God promises that what comes against us will not become what it was created to be. Anything that comes against us will always fall short of its original intent.

Falling short of the goal is exactly what the enemy tries to convince us to do in the in-between. This is where we hear that we're too much or not enough in some way, shape, or form. This is where we are tempted to give up or turn away, but it will not work. We will not shrink back. We will be big. We will be bold. We will be women whose faith has preserved our souls. We are women who breathe the breath of victory every moment because the Holy Spirit breathes through us. The victory doesn't come without a fight, but we are made to flourish in the hard places. Our flourishing isn't only for us either. We were made to lead the way so that others could walk a well-worn path. As the Holy Spirit softens our hearts, we begin to stand on the neck of the enemy. We reclaim our authority and our anointing. Our flourishing ushers in deliverance both for ourselves and for others. We will see chains break in the lives of those around us as our flourishing jumpstarts their own.

Heavenly Father, I pray that You would unveil within us the unlimited riches of Your glory and favor until supernatural strength floods our innermost beings with Your divine might and explosive power. Then, by constantly using our faith, we pray that the life of Christ will be released deep inside us, and the resting place of His love will become the very source and root of our lives. (Eph. 3:16-17, TPT) In the mighty name of Jesus, our Lord and Savior, we pray. Amen.

Reflect

. . .

Where do you need to remember that those weapons that come against you cannot flourish?

_____

_____

_____

_____

_____

_____

What if your individual "breaking forth" is directly tied to the territory you take from the enemy for years to come?

_____

_____

_____

_____

_____

Where is that hard, uncertain place that the Holy Spirit is telling you to flourish this week?

_____

_____

_____

_____

_____

_____

Dancing in the Valley of Baca

• • •

Psalm 84:4b–7a (AMP)

They will be singing Your praises all the day long. Selah. Blessed and greatly favored is the man [or woman] whose strength is in You, [i]n whose heart are the highways to Zion. Passing through the Valley of Weeping (Baca), they make it a place of springs; The early rain also covers it with blessings. They go from strength to strength [increasing in victorious power].

Isaiah 43:19 (NIV)

"See, I am doing a new thing! Now it springs up; do you not perceive it? I am making a way in the wilderness and streams in the wasteland."

I WOKE UP IN the middle of the night a few months ago and wrote the words "my daughters will dance in the Valley of Baca" on a piece of paper. I didn't even know what the Valley of Baca was! This was just a phrase the Lord put on my heart, so of course, I had to find out why it was so important. Also called the Valley of Weeping, it is only mentioned once in the entire Bible and is believed to be a literal valley that the Jewish people traveled through on their way to Jerusalem. It was named Valley of Baca because the trees that grew there dripped ("wept") sap. It is a dead, arid wasteland. Many believe that the Valley of Baca is located about 2.5–4.35 miles just outside of the Old City of Jerusalem. It's only about an hour's walk. This means it was one of the very last places Israelites passed through before reaching Jerusalem. For us, the Valley of Baca can be a place of sorrow or simply a place of dry, arid nothingness just outside of our Promised Land. If we've arrived here in the in-between, it means we're actually on the right road, even though it definitely doesn't look like it!

We are passing through the Valley of Baca in the in-between—never camping out or staying there. We must remind ourselves that we are blessed and greatly favored women as we go through this place, regardless of what we feel. We must remind ourselves that our God is faithful, despite the arid wasteland that we see before us. The Valley of Baca can be a place of refreshment as the Lord creates springs in the desert here. We have to remember to still sing praises to God in this place as we lean on His strength and not our own. As tough as it is to walk through, it is a landmark letting us know that we are just outside the fulfillment of our promises.

It's part of the in-between but it's also a place of transformation. I have found that the Lord can lead us through this arid land in such a way that we're able to dance upon the very ground that used to be soaked with our tears. Mourning turns to supernatural joy. We begin to see pieces of our stories redeemed in the lives of those around us. We begin to experience the Holy Spirit using our lives to set others free and we become thankful for it all. We realize that nothing has been wasted. We finally believe that there are no tears that have gone unseen. We find sacred purposes in the pain. We begin to grasp that joy is being and will be repaid for every sorrow, and it will truly be glorious. This valley becomes a gift as we watch the Lord take every hard, dry place and turn it into streams overflowing with goodness and restoration. We dance because this is where we experience the goodness of God in the land of the living. The tears we've sown become the water that allows beautiful new flowers to spring up across our paths. Keep walking. We are exactly where we are supposed to be on our way to victory!

Almighty God, thank You that this is a place filled with blessings, even when it all looks dry or forgotten around us. Thank You, Abba, that we are on the right road! We are so in awe of how You love to create some-

thing out of nothing. Thank You, Lord, for the early rain! We ask, Lord, that You would take all our places of nothingness and make streams in the desert. We are women who will not just pass through but increase our faith. We rejoice that we are overcomers. We are more victorious with every step. Thank You, Holy Spirit, for working in and through us to transform us into women who dance on the soil that was watered with our tears. Only You, God, only You. Open our eyes to see the springs that have already begun in this place. We give You all the glory today in Jesus's mighty name. Amen!

Reflect

. . .

Have you ever felt like you were in the Valley of Baca? What happened while you were there?

_____

_____

_____

_____

_____

_____

_____

_____

_____

How have you seen the hand of the Lord move upon your life in this place?

_____

_____

_____

_____

_____

_____

_____

_____

Where do you need the Lord to encourage you with the knowledge that you're at the doorstep of your Promised Land?

_____

_____

_____

_____

_____

_____

_____

_____

_____

Where have you acted like this place is one to wallow in instead of one to pass through?

_____

_____

_____

_____

_____

_____

_____

_____

_____

_____

WEEK 48

Listen for the Rain

• • •

1 Kings 18:1 (ESV)
After many days the word of the Lord came to Elijah, in the third year, saying, "Go, show yourself to Ahab, and I will send rain upon the earth."

1 Kings 18:41 (MSG)
Elijah said to Ahab, "Up on your feet! Eat and drink—celebrate! Rain is on the way; I hear [emphasis added] it coming."

FIRST KINGS 18 starts with "[a]fter many days" or "[a] long time passed." That might as well have been written today—basically, it's been so long that the days blur together and no one wants to talk about how long it's been. The drought had been going on for three years. Three years of the people waiting for God to answer their prayers. Three years of hoping. Three years of desperate cries. Three years of watching and seeing nothing. And then when Elijah did start praying, his servant looked at the sky six times and saw absolutely nothing. We know what that feels like. In fact, doing that in our own lives can be downright discouraging. But we miss that it all started with listening, not seeing.

Several years ago, I was in Karamoja—a remote village in Uganda. Although most of Uganda is lush, Karamoja is not. Rain is almost nonexistent, so the ground is dry and cracked, hard as cement. On my last day, I looked up and saw dark clouds in the distance. Because it had been so long, I could hear and feel the rain in the ground under me. It echoed with a thunderous noise, welcoming the blessing it had desperately waited for. It was like the earth was announcing that something great was coming, long before that rain actually reached the place where I stood. While Elijah heard the rain in his spirit first, experiencing this in Africa gave me a whole new perspective on these verses.

We know to praise the Lord when the blessing arrives, but to tell someone to get up, eat, drink, and celebrate before anything's happened seems ridiculous. To celebrate when nothing's changed just doesn't even make sense. And yet, that's what we are called to do. That's where faith expands. That's where expectation grows to make room for the power of the Holy Spirit to enter in. When we give the Lord glory before the breakthrough, it ensures that we give the Lord glory after the breakthrough. We are never asked to understand. The Lord only ever asks us to believe. We don't read that as the empowered command that it is. Think of the prayers you've been waiting to see answered or promises that haven't come to pass. Each one echoes a deep hope, ache, plea, or desperate cry to God. That is the dry ground of Karamoja. And that is where Elijah says to celebrate and listen for the rain. So, beautiful ones, get up, take care of yourselves, and celebrate because it's time to praise the Lord in advance for the rain that's about to pour all over our lives.

Heavenly Father, thank You for stretching our faith in this season. Thank You for giving us the opportunity to lean into Your still, small voice and hold tighter to Your promises. Thank You for using the situations around us to transform us. We remain confident that we will see the goodness of the Lord in the land of the living. Thank You for reminding us today of Your faithfulness, Father God; Your Word never returns void. You do not fail to act after You speak. What You have promised, You will fulfill. We trust in, rely on, and are confident in You, Lord. We are Your daughters, and we are listening. We are available and want to be used mightily by You. We say, "Yes, Abba!" Our times are in Your hands. We believe, God, that You are working. We celebrate You today, Lord. Help us to listen for Your rain in our lives, Jesus. Amen.

Reflect

• • •

Where have you celebrated God's faithfulness before you can see what He's doing?

_____

_____

_____

_____

_____

_____

_____

_____

_____

_____

Do you pray knowing that even if you have to check 6, 10, 15, 20, 40 times that if God has promised it, He will surely do it? Why or why not?

_____

_____

_____

_____

_____

_____

_____

_____

_____

Where have you been quiet enough to listen to the blessing that's on the way?

_____

_____

_____

_____

_____

_____

_____

_____

_____

Where have you only noticed God's interventions once they become life's interruptions?

_____

_____

_____

_____

_____

_____

_____

_____

_____

_____

Get Excited

. . .

Psalm 37:4 (ESV)
Delight yourselves in the Lord, and he will give you the desires of your heart.

Matthew 22:37 (NIV)
Jesus replied: "Love the Lord your God with all your heart and with all your soul and with all your mind."

RECENTLY, THE HOLY Spirit whispered to my heart, "Get excited." My first thought was "For what?" and my second thought was "Why is it so important to God that I'm excited about this?" I didn't have an answer. Then yesterday morning, I was at a restaurant when across from me I heard a little girl say, "Abba! Abba!" She was pulling on her dad's shirt, so excited to talk to him about whatever was important to her. He was engrossed in another conversation, so it took her about five or six "Abbas" to get his attention. But when he turned to her, his eyes lit up as he gave her his full, completely undivided attention. You could tell how happy he was in her delight and how happy she was to have his face turned towards her.

A friend of mine last night told me, "I want to live less from my head and more from my heart, but how do I do that?" Part of what she was experiencing was hope deferred—something she's prayed about for so long that hasn't come to pass yet. So, we talked about the importance of getting excited and shaking off the weariness by approaching our Heavenly Father eager to spend time with Him. We also have to be excitedly expectant about what He's promised because He *will* turn His face towards us!

Do we approach God with eagerness and enthusiasm—as that little girl did with her father? Do we pray with excitement and enthusiasm, expecting God to turn His face to us? I'll admit that there have been seasons when my quiet time with the Lord has been more because I know I need to and much less childlike excitement. But our Heavenly Father desires our childlike joy! If only we came to our Abba with the same excitement that we have when approaching an upcoming vacation, or our favorite sports team, or even our favorite dessert. When we are excited about something, we approach it with *hope, gratitude,* and *joy.*

God longs to turn His face to us and get wrapped up in all of the delight that resides in the desires of our hearts. This is not being optimistic. This is being realistic about exactly how much and how deeply we matter. This is about a God that spreads signs and wonders across the skies of our lives. Our joy is a big deal to Him. In fact, God's pursuit of glory and our pursuit of joy should be so intertwined that they are the same pursuit. Freedom in Christ and the outpouring of His glory is the deep work of our hearts. God is moving and we don't want to miss what He's about to do next. Start today by letting the Holy Spirit stir up enthusiasm about who He is and what He's done while we get ready for what's to come.

Abba, Jesus, Holy Spirit, stir up our hearts! We want more of You and less of ourselves. We want to come to You jumping up and down with joy—saying "Abba! Abba! Abba!" out of the overflow of our hearts. While everything in this world tells us to despair, You speak hope and tell us to get excited! Show us, Holy Spirit, a specific area that each of us can be excited about today. Show us each where You are lighting a fire in our hearts and where You have much more to come. We want to delight in You, Lord and reflect that delight to everyone around us. We pray that those we come into contact with would see such a change in us. Let the difference be more of Your Holy Spirit moving in our lives! You are beyond all we can ask, think, or imagine. Abba, we love You. In the mighty name of Jesus, we pray. Amen.

Reflect

. . .

Are you expecting God to amaze you, or are you subconsciously putting limits on His goodness?

_____

_____

_____

_____

_____

_____

Are you truly delighting in the Lord, eager to spend time with Him? Why or why not?

_____

_____

_____

_____

_____

Where do you need the Holy Spirit to stir excitement up in your heart?

_____

_____

_____

_____

_____

WEEK 50

A New Song to Sing

• • •

Psalm 40:3 (AMP)
He put a new song in my mouth, a song of praise to our God; [m]any will see and fear [with great reverence] [a]nd will trust confidently in the Lord.

Revelation 5:9–10 (ESV)
And they sang a new song, saying, "Worthy are You to take the scroll and to open its seals, for you were slain, and by your blood you ransomed people for God from every tribe and language and people and nation, and you have made them a kingdom and priests to our God, and they shall reign on the earth."

"I AM GIVING YOU a new song to sing." This is something that the Holy Spirit has whispered into my heart multiple times this year. When I researched what it means to sing a new song, I realized that this is all over the Bible. Clearly, this is something that's important to God because it's repeated multiple times, but what does it really mean to have a new song to sing? What does that new song sound like?

When we are given a new song to sing, it is a fresh song of praise—for who God is and what He is doing (or will do). It's a song of salvation, a song of deliverance, a song of joy, a song of redemption, and it's different for each one of us. Thinking over the past couple of years, my song has been one of tremendous healing, wholeness, provision, and protection. But that's now my old song. Both the old song (of remembrance) and the new song have value, but the Lord is teaching me a new song now. He doesn't have to remind us to sing the old songs. We know how they go and can recall them. The same way that we know the lyrics to familiar songs on the radio, the old songs of our lives become etched in our minds and on our hearts.

I believe the Lord is giving many of His daughters new songs to sing in this season. A song of victory. A tune of deliverance. A melody of thankfulness. A sway of joy and dance of deeper love. Beginning to walk out of the in-between season creates a new song of praise on our lips. Experiencing mighty moves of the Holy Spirit in ways we haven't before gives us a new song to sing. Beginning to watch everything that the Lord promised come to pass definitely gives us a new song to sing. The song is a new way of the Lord revealing Himself to us. One day, we will know all the lyrics by heart, but for now, it's a song of praise that we learn as we go. Fortunately, we have a master conductor who will put the new music in our mouths and the words to sing. It's time to dance and sing and shout for joy. It's time to let the Holy Spirit teach us a new song for this new season that's unfolding.

Heavenly Father, thank You that You have promised You will give us new songs to sing. A song of praise and adoration to You. Thank You for the old songs that we remember as we celebrate how mighty, how majestic, and how incomparable You are. Thank You for all the ways You are preparing us for what You have prepared for us. We pray, Father God, that by Your Holy Spirit, You'd show us the incomparable riches of Your grace in a new way, through Your kindness to us in Christ Jesus. We desire to know so much more of You. You promise that You will give to those who ask, seek, and knock, so we ask for more of You. We seek new songs to sing and new opportunities to praise You, and we knock with all of our strength—knowing You will answer in the mighty, matchless name of Jesus. Amen.

Reflect

• • •

How would your circumstances change if you approached each day with a new song to sing in your heart?

_____

_____

_____

_____

_____

_____

_____

_____

What if this little taste of heaven came to the earth? How would your songs vary and blend?

_____

_____

_____

_____

_____

_____

_____

_____

What new song is the Lord giving you to sing in this season?

_____

_____

_____

_____

_____

_____

_____

_____

_____

How can you start stepping forward to live this new song out?

_____

_____

_____

_____

_____

_____

_____

_____

_____

_____

WEEK 51

Prepared for Yes

. . .

Esther 5:4–5 (MSG)
"If it please the king," said Esther, "let the king come with Haman to a dinner I've prepared for him." "Get Haman at once," said the king, "so we can go to dinner with Esther."

Mark 16:1–4 (NIV)
When the Sabbath was over, Mary Magdalene, Mary the mother of James, and Salome bought spices so that they might go anoint Jesus' body. Very early on the first day of the week, just after sunrise, they were on their way to the tomb and they asked each other, "Who will roll the stone away from the entrance of the tomb?" But when they looked up, they saw that the stone, which was very large, had been rolled away.

THERE'S A THEME in these verses that the Lord put on my heart this week. In both cases, the women prepared and walked in faith as if they had already received their yes. In Esther's case, she had prepared dinner for the king and Haman before she even approached the king. She had a banquet ready before he held out his gold scepter to let her speak and had planned for a second yes before the king even accepted her invitation to dinner. What bold faith! Esther didn't know if she would live, let alone if the king would come to dinner two nights in a row.

In the case of Jesus, the women had bought spices and were heading up to Jesus's tomb before they knew how they'd even get in to reach the body. They didn't know how they'd actually reach the body with the large stone in front of the tomb, but they went anyway. In both cases, it was good that the women were prepared because the answer was not only yes but also a sudden yes. Suddenly, the king rushed to Esther's dinner (with Haman). Suddenly the stone was rolled away, so the women could enter the tomb and be the first ones in the Bible to know that Jesus is risen.

Here's the thing: God never fails. Never. So *when* the Lord says yes and that situation changes, or that loved one comes home, or that disease is healed, then what? Are we actually ready for the Lord to give us the thing that we've been praying for? Because seasons are changing, and how we walk out of the in-between is just as important as how we enter into it. Will we be like the seven Israelite tribes of Joshua 18 who were *in* the Promised Land but still hadn't taken possession of it? Or will we not only enter in but also get established in our inheritance?

I believe that there are some specific things that the Lord is asking each of us to prepare for and move forward in as if we've already heard our *yes*. If that dream job or that new home suddenly became available, could we take hold of that opportunity? Are we living our lives in the faith of Esther? Are we prepared for the promise that's about to unfold behind the obstacles in front of us like Mary Magdalene, Mary, and Salome?

Almighty God, we thank You that Your promises are Yes and Amen. Thank You, Lord, for the honor of preparing us for the sudden yeses that You have for us. Thank You for Your Word that shows us the importance of walking in our yes before we see it. Help us, Holy Spirit, to see and hear You more clearly—that we may be led only by Your Spirit. Silence the idle words and noise around us in Jesus's name. We believe You are a good, good Father, Who gives good and perfect gifts to Your children. We believe You are the Alpha and the Omega, the beginning and the end. We pray, Lord, that You would show us each the specific step of faith to take for the yes we each are believing for. We love You and we need You every moment of every day. In Jesus's Name. Amen.

Reflect

. . .

Which story can you relate to more—Esther's or the three women at the tomb and why?

_____

_____

_____

_____

_____

_____

Where are you asking the Lord to say yes?

_____

_____

_____

_____

_____

What specific action or step of faith can you take this week to be better prepared for your yes?

_____

_____

_____

_____

_____

When God Remembers

. . .

Genesis 8:1 (NRSV)
But God remembered Noah and all the wild animals and all the domestic animals that were with him in the ark. And God made a wind blow over the earth, and the waters subsided.

Genesis 30:22 (NRSV)
Then God remembered Rachel, and God heeded her and opened her womb.

WHAT DOES IT mean when God remembers? It's not like God forgot that Noah and his family were the only people left on earth during the flood, right? Or that Rachel and Hannah had both been barren for years? The Lord sees every tear, hears every cry, and does not forget His children. God does not have lapses of memory or judgment. We are engraved on the palms of the Lord's hands and cannot, will not, ever be forgotten. So why does the Bible say that "God remembered"?

The Old Testament word for "remember" is the Hebrew word, *zakar*, which not only means to bring to mind but also, more importantly, to act on that person's behalf. So, it's more along the lines of the Lord recalling the prayers of His children and then doing something about it. Every instance of God remembering in the Bible also includes an action. The flood waters receded when the Lord remembered Noah. Rachel and Hannah both conceived when the Lord remembered them. The Israelites were rescued out of slavery in Egypt when the Lord remembered. I believe that it's because of this that David in Psalm 25 asks the Lord to "remember" him. He's not asking the Lord to mentally recall him per se. He's asking God to act on his behalf out of the abundance of His goodness and mercy.

When God remembers, the atmosphere shifts. Promises manifest. Healing occurs. The wind blows to reveal solid ground. Hope is renewed. Freedom arrives. Chains break. Waters part. When God remembers us, our lives change forever. It's a moment of suddenly that's years in the making. It's the prodigal coming home. It's new life and new love bursting forth. It's when we finally hold in our hands that which has only been carried in our hearts. It's a precious thing, and it's a sign that we are shifting into a new season. As God remembered His people, each time it culminated in the end of one thing and the beginning of something else. The earth was no longer covered in a flood. Hannah and Rachel were no longer barren. The Israelites were no longer slaves in Egypt.

The Lord redefines who we are as He remembers us. We are changed in order to walk into the next place and the open space that has been prepared while we're in the in-between. This is a moment of celebration! As we hold with thankfulness where we've been, we know it's time to step into the new.

Almighty God, thank You that You have remembered Your children throughout the Bible and You are remembering us today. Thank You for engraving us on the palms of Your hands so that our names, our promises, our prayers, and our thanksgivings are never forgotten. Heavenly Father, we ask today that You would remember us once more. Holy Spirit, You've heard the cries of our hearts and positioned us well for the new thing You are doing. We ask, Lord Jesus, that You would unfold that now and allow us to see You work! May we be amazed by all that You are doing and all that You are going to do. We praise You, Lord, and we thank You that You are moving on our behalf now in Jesus's name! Amen.

Reflect

. . .

What does it mean to you "when God remembers"?

_____

_____

_____

_____

_____

_____

What comes to mind when you think of times when the Lord has remembered you in the past?

_____

_____

_____

_____

_____

_____

In what areas of life are you believing for the Lord to remember you this week?

_____

_____

_____

_____

_____

_____

Acknowledgements

. . .

THERE ARE SO many people who have spoken life into this project and without whom it never would've come together. Since this is a women's devotional, I'd like to highlight some of the women that the Lord has used greatly in this.

First, to my prayer warrior sisters—Dawn, Gina, Brooke, Dawnielle, Heidi-Marie, and Tara, you all convinced me that the Lord had given me something beautiful and worthy of sharing with other women. You kept checking in on "the book" and encouraged me to keep going every time I wanted to say this process was too hard or too long. Thank you, thank you, thank you.

To Jennifer, Christa, Danielle, Bre, Jenna, Alice, Laurie, Nicole, Elissa, Christina, Lisa, Brenda, Christine, and Virginia—thank you for being part of the small group of trustworthy encouragers who have held this book close to your own hearts over the last year. Thank you for constantly reminding me of the importance of my obedience in this.

To my Galilee Church family, I simply would not be where I am as a Christian woman if it weren't for you. Thank you for introducing me to the Holy Spirit, walking alongside me during the craziest of times, growing my faith, and always lifting me up with your prayers. Thank you will never be enough. I know that I am who I am because you all have taught and led so well.

To Lisa & Jodie—thank you for being such incredible examples of godly women. Your unwavering faith and excitement for the Lord showed me who I wanted to be. Thank you for always letting me dig into your DVDs and endless selection of Christian books to learn all I could in my early Christian walk. You have been more life-giving than you know.

To my Bel Air Church family, you are where my deepest healing began. You immediately welcomed me into your church when I was a stranger in Los Angeles. I know without a doubt that I would not be whole or healed without the safety and love of this community. I can't imagine missing out on the redemptive work that the Lord has done through you all in my life over the last few years, not to mention the sheer miracles I've witnessed. I have no doubt that what's next will be simply tremendous!

To Rebecca and Carrie, thank you for always being ready to speak life and love hard. You both are such beautiful examples of courage and grace. Be big.

To Karen and the Hollywood Prayer Network family, you are tremendous. I am so lucky to call you a mentor and friend. Thank you for your continued wisdom and encouragement in so many areas of life, not just in this book.

To Connie and Kathryn, this is a Jesus thing. Thank you so much for your Spirit-filled prophetic words and prayers. They helped me push through to the end of this process exactly when I needed them. Thank you for both being such tremendous examples of what it looks like to obey the Lord, no matter what that looks like to anyone else.

Finally, to Mom, Dad, Elizabeth, Nick, Walter, and Emily—I love you all beyond measure and am so thankful that God gave me each one of you to call family.